Advance praise for *Those Seve*

"The Bible has been used as a bludgeon against LGBTQ persons for far too long. Thus, the most frequent question I get from those who are coming to terms with their sexual orientation or that of a child or loved one is to please explain to them how this could be OK when the Bible appears to be so 'clear' in its condemnation. This fine and easily accessible book offers what the Apostle Paul has called 'a more excellent way' that reads the Bible in terms of love rather than hate, hope rather than fear."

—Mark Wingfield, Executive Director and Publisher, Baptist News Global, and author of *Why Churches Need to Talk About Sexuality*

"John Dwyer masterfully navigates the reader through a biblical journey of re-discovery as he delves deeply into the seven historical references used as 'clobber' texts against LGBTQIA+ inclusion. This is a must-read not only for the LGBTQIA+ community but also for anyone who seeks to be an ally in the building of the Beloved Community."

—The Rt. Rev. Deon K. Johnson, Eleventh Bishop of Missouri

"For generations, seven biblical texts have been used to deny LGBTQ their dignity and humanity as children of God. In this careful scholarly work, John Dwyer provides preachers, pastors, and Christians wrestling with these texts new ways to understand their full meaning and challenge their misuse. This valuable volume will help Episcopalians speak out when the Bible is used to attack our LGBTQ siblings in Christ."

—The Rev. Gay Clark Jennings, President, House of Deputies of the Episcopal Church

THOSE 7 REFERENCES

THOSE 7 REFERENCES

A STUDY OF THE REFERENCES TO "HOMOSEXUALITY" IN THE BIBLE AND THEIR IMPACT ON THE QUEER COMMUNITY OF FAITH

JOHN F. DWYER

Morehouse Publishing, 19 East 34th Street, New York, NY 10016

Morehouse Publishing is an imprint of Church Publishing Incorporated.
www.churchpublishing.org

Cover design by Jennifer Kopec, 2Pug Design
Interior design and typesetting by Beth Oberholtzer

Library of Congress Cataloging-in-Publication Data

Names: Dwyer, John F., Rev., author.
Title: Those seven references : a study of the references to "homosexuality" in the Bible and their impact on the queer community of faith / John F. Dwyer.
Identifiers: LCCN 2020046717 (print) | LCCN 2020046718 (ebook) | ISBN 9781640653375 (paperback) | ISBN 9781640653382 (epub)
Subjects: LCSH: Homosexuality--Biblical teaching. | Bible--Criticism, interpretation, etc.
Classification: LCC BS680.H67 D89 2021 (print) | LCC BS680.H67 (ebook) | DDC 220.8/306766--dc23
LC record available at https://lccn.loc.gov/2020046717
LC ebook record available at https://lccn.loc.gov/2020046718

CONTENTS

FOREWORD

Over a decade ago I penned a scholarly, exegetical work exploring passages in the Bible that have been and continue to be used as tools of repression and abuse toward queer individuals. The original work was written prior to the progress in LGBTQ+ rights achieved over the course of the last twelve years. Enormous strides toward equality for the queer community have been made in that time. Concurrently, there have also been regressive local-legislative actions seeking to limit those national steps toward equality. Many of those who have led these regressive efforts are individuals steeped in purposeful ignorance, bias, tribalism, and a radicalization of faithful beliefs, misleading their congregations and influencing legislators. These efforts have drawn me to revise and update the original work, because these verses continue to be misused.

Whether straight, lesbian, gay, transgender, nonbinary, celibate, or any other blessed manifestation of God's creation, the exploration in this project is meant to provide words to describe how God's love is present to all of God's creation, and to provide language and understanding that these passages are not focused on queer people. Personhood, the intense value of our individuality, cannot be made less by these passages of scripture: God's love for our uniqueness is not compromised by oft misinterpreted verses. My hope is that this study may provide understanding, knowledge, and words to express that God's love is for all of us, no matter who we are and how we identify. We are loved just as God created us.

Finally, I want to thank my husband, Ben, for proofreading, and my editor at Church Publishing, Milton Basher-Cunningham, whose insights and patient editing have made this work better and more readable.

JFD+
Berkeley, California, 2019

ACKNOWLEDGMENTS

There are many people to whom I want to give thanks for their assistance and inspiration in creation of this work. My advisors on the project, Dr. Judy Fentriss-Williams and The Very Rev. Dr. Lloyd A. Lewis, whose sage wisdom, patience, advice, and counsel allowed me the freedom to research and find a voice in which the dialogue in and between different scriptural passages could be explored. I want to thank the institution that is Virginia Theological Seminary, which has allowed me a place to be formed as an ordained person and to explore and hear God's Word. The Rev. Dr. Roger Ferlo and the Rev. Dr. Nancy Lee Jose, both who as priests, rectors, and teachers have provided support, guidance, and love throughout this journey, and to whom I owe a debt of gratitude far in excess of these words. All the people at my sponsoring parish in New York City, St. Luke in the Fields, and the folks at my field education parish in Washington. DC, St. Thomas' Parish, have inspired me to do this research and look for a voice with which to better understand passages of scripture which have been used as weapons of violence against tender souls. Finally, I want to thank my friends who supported me this past year, encouraging me with their interest, questions, and love.

INTRODUCTION

I firmly believe that the Bible is the living and breathing word of God. God's self-revelatory word shows God's yearning to be in relationship with us as evident in our creation and the Incarnation of Jesus. Yet relationships are two-way streets. So the Bible and our study of it are also signs of our yearning to be in relationship and conversation with God. The Bible is one of the ways we get to know God and God gets to know us.

If the Bible is the living and breathing word of God, then as with anything in this world that is alive, thriving, and well, there must be growth or else stagnation sets in and that living thing will die. Our understanding of God's Word to us grows as we, as human beings, develop and grow. To be the living, breathing words of God, these texts must be made understandable to each succeeding generation that hears them for the first time.

One of the basic tenets of the Anglican tradition, of which The Episcopal Church is a part, is that our faith is understood and distilled through the "three-legged stool" of scripture, tradition, and reason; each leg of that stool being equal and as important as the other. As with any stool, if one leg becomes out of kilter with any other, the stool will wobble and fall over.

There are many ways of interpreting and understanding the Bible. Some believe that a literal approach is the only lens through which scripture should be read. By looking at the Bible through this singular and literal lens, the meaning of the Bible can be misconstrued, and thereby tilt that three-legged stool. We need multiple lenses through which the Bible can be studied and understood. Looking at these texts from different angles, through different lenses, provides a broader perspective. These different ways of understanding the texts inform a more nuanced and conversant way to engage with scripture.

The Bible as we know it was written over the course of centuries, lovingly passed down from generation to generation with alterations, modifications, additions, and subtractions made to these words of God. Those that take these words of God and try to freeze them in a translational context do a disservice to those engaging with those texts, which can thwart God's present voice being heard.

A literal lens can also miss the broader point and story that the information around a passage is setting forth: simply stated, taking something out of context and utilizing it for one's own purposes perverts the message being presented. Therefore, it is important to read, at a minimum, the whole chapter surrounding the verses under study to understand what is being relayed by the authors and editors of the texts. This method assists in not taking things out of context and will provide a deeper interaction with those texts.

The studies of the various passages which follow attempt to look at these passages in context with those that are around them, as well as to demonstrate how they fit into the more global aspect of the canon which has been passed down to us; to understand the language utilized in the original manuscripts; to review the nuances of those words and what they meant to the people at the time they were written, and in some cases rewritten and edited; to review how these passages have been interpreted and understood throughout the generations that have worshipped with them; to review any different translations and understandings of particular words; and to look at how these passages are applicable to our current society and world. This approach is firmly entrenched in the three-legged stool approach to understanding theology and the Bible: basing the understanding of the passage in question on tradition, scripture, and reason.

The starting point for all discussions in this work will be the New Revised Standard Bible translation (NRSV). Other translations will be utilized for comparison purposes and will be specifically identified.

A word of warning: some of the anthropological concepts, societal understandings, and discussions which follow may be difficult to read for some due to the graphic and personal nature of what these passages under review focus on: sex and sexual relations. In order to understand these passages, the sociocultural understanding of sex and sexual relations at the time the passages were written must be understood. Thus, they are explored in the following pages.

This study is meant to add another voice to the ongoing discussion of the place of LGBTQ+ persons in the experience and life of the Church. This work is by no means exhaustive or all-encompassing. My dream is to give voice, hope, understanding, and words to counter bias to those who have been abused by the misuse of scripture, allowing God's voice to be heard in these passages in ways that have been silenced for many queer people—to be another voice in the continuing conversation about and with God, and to provide in one place the direct biblical references to homosexuality.

CHAPTER ONE

Genesis 19 AND Judges 19

Part One: Genesis 19

The two angels came to Sodom in the evening, and Lot was
sitting in the gateway of Sodom. When Lot saw them, he rose
to meet them, and bowed down with his face to the ground.
2 He said, “Please, my lords, turn aside to your servant’s house
and spend the night, and wash your feet; then you can rise early
and go on your way.” They said, “No; we will spend the night
in the square.” 3 But he urged them strongly; so they turned
aside to him and entered his house; and he made them a feast,
and baked unleavened bread, and they ate. 4 But before they
lay down, the men of the city, the men of Sodom, both young
and old, all the people to the last man, surrounded the house;
5 and they called to Lot, “Where are the men who came to you
tonight? Bring them out to us, so that we may know them.”
6 Lot went out of the door to the men, shut the door after him,
7 and said, “I beg you, my brothers, do not act so wickedly.
8 Look, I have two daughters who have not known a man; let

me bring them out to you, and do to them as you please; only
do nothing to these men, for they have come under the shelter
of my roof." 9 But they replied, "Stand back!" And they said,
"This fellow came here as an alien, and he would play the
judge! Now we will deal worse with you than with them."
Then they pressed hard against the man Lot, and came near
the door to break it down. 10 But the men inside reached out
their hands and brought Lot into the house with them, and shut
the door. 11 And they struck with blindness the men who were
at the door of the house, both small and great, so that they were
unable to find the door. 12 Then the men said to Lot, "Have you
anyone else here? Sons-in-law, sons, daughters, or anyone you
have in the city—bring them out of the place. 13 For we are
about to destroy this place, because the outcry against its
people has become great before the LORD, and the LORD
has sent us to destroy it." 14 So Lot went out and said to his
sons-in-law, who were to marry his daughters, "Up, get out
of this place; for the LORD is about to destroy the city." But
he seemed to his sons-in-law to be jesting. 15 When morning
dawned, the angels urged Lot, saying, "Get up, take your wife
and your two daughters who are here, or else you will be
consumed in the punishment of the city." 16 But he lingered;
so the men seized him and his wife and his two daughters by
the hand, the LORD being merciful to him, and they brought
him out and left him outside the city. 17 When they had brought
them outside, they said, "Flee for your life; do not look back or
stop anywhere in the Plain; flee to the hills, or else you will be
consumed." 18 And Lot said to them, "Oh, no, my lords; 19 your
servant has found favor with you, and you have shown me great
kindness in saving my life; but I cannot flee to the hills, for fear

the disaster will overtake me and I die. [20] Look, that city is near
enough to flee to, and it is a little one. Let me escape there—
is it not a little one?—and my life will be saved!" [21] He said to
him, "Very well, I grant you this favor too, and will not overthrow the city of which you have spoken. [22] Hurry, escape
there, for I can do nothing until you arrive there." Therefore
the city was called Zoar. [23] The sun had risen on the earth
when Lot came to Zoar. [24] Then the LORD rained on Sodom
and Gomorrah sulfur and fire from the LORD out of heaven;
[25] and he overthrew those cities, and all the Plain, and all the
inhabitants of the cities, and what grew on the ground. [26] But
Lot's wife, behind him, looked back, and she became a pillar
of salt. [27] Abraham went early in the morning to the place
where he had stood before the LORD; [28] and he looked down
toward Sodom and Gomorrah and toward all the land of the
Plain and saw the smoke of the land going up like the smoke
of a furnace. [29] So it was that, when God destroyed the cities
of the Plain, God remembered Abraham, and sent Lot out of
the midst of the overthrow, when he overthrew the cities in
which Lot had settled. [30] Now Lot went up out of Zoar and
settled in the hills with his two daughters, for he was afraid
to stay in Zoar; so he lived in a cave with his two daughters.
[31] And the firstborn said to the younger, "Our father is old, and
there is not a man on earth to come in to us after the manner
of all the world. [32] Come, let us make our father drink wine,
and we will lie with him, so that we may preserve offspring
through our father." [33] So they made their father drink wine that
night; and the firstborn went in, and lay with her father; he did
not know when she lay down or when she rose. [34] On the next
day, the firstborn said to the younger, "Look, I lay last night

> with my father; let us make him drink wine tonight also; then
> you go in and lie with him, so that we may preserve offspring
> through our father." [35] So they made their father drink wine that
> night also; and the younger rose, and lay with him; and he did
> not know when she lay down or when she rose. [36] Thus both
> the daughters of Lot became pregnant by their father. [37] The
> firstborn bore a son, and named him Moab; he is the ancestor
> of the Moabites to this day. [38] The younger also bore a son and
> named him Ben-ammi; he is the ancestor of the Ammonites
> to this day.

Reading this chapter of Genesis on its own while ignoring what surrounds it can lead to an interpretation that misconstrues the complex interweaving of the story of Lot and Sodom and Gomorrah with the larger Abrahamic story that surrounds this chapter. An important concept to understand at the beginning of this discussion is that this tale of Lot and the town in which he lives falls right in the middle of the account of Abraham.[1] In biblical interpretation, this is often referred to as "sandwiching:" where a seemingly disjointed and unconnected narrative interrupts what appears to be the natural flow of the story. When this occurs, the reader should pause and reflect why the flow of the narrative has been interrupted. Abraham is absent from the story of Lot until verse 27, when he reappears to look silently at the destruction wrought by God on Sodom and Gomorrah. What initially appears to be an interruption is an integral part of the larger story of Abraham.

The story of Lot and how he greets and treats the guests to his city has important parallels to what transpired just prior to this story. Genesis 18 and 19, taken together, offer the most comprehensive twenty-four-hour time span in the life of Abraham that is found in the Bible, with the story of Lot illuminating God's expectations of Abraham and all of God's people.[2]

To understand properly the import of Lot's behavior and that of the townsfolk of Sodom, I offer a brief outline of the events of chapter 18. Abraham is found sitting at the entrance of his tent, hiding from the heat of the day, when he sees three men standing not far from him. He runs to them, bows deeply, and makes an offer of water to wash their feet, shade in which they might rest, and bread for them to eat. Abraham identifies one of these men as "lord," alerting the reader that these are no ordinary men. Abraham is seen hustling around, asking Sarah to make cakes from the finest flour and taking a choice calf, which is described as "tender and good." He prepares curd and then brings all these things to the guests for them to eat while he stands by and watches.

The guests then ask about Sarah, who overhears the promise that a son shall be provided "in due season," at which point Sarah laughs and then denies her laughter. But one of the visitors corrects her lie and repeats God's promise of a son. Then the men leave the tent area and go to look at Sodom. A remarkable passage then begins where the reader hears God's inner debate about whether to tell Abraham of the fate of Sodom. God decides to tell Abraham because he is God's chosen one. God says that "all the nations of the earth shall be blessed in him" (18:18) and that through Abraham these nations shall learn "righteousness and justice" (18:19). God then tells Abraham of the plan to destroy Sodom because of an unspecified wickedness. Abraham begins bargaining with God over the fate of Sodom and the punishment of the righteous with the unrighteous. At the end of this bargaining, God promises that should ten righteous individuals be found in the town, God will not destroy it.

After the negotiation between Abraham and God, the chapter ends and "the Lord went his way . . . and Abraham returned to his place." The Sodom saga then begins in chapter 19, with

Abraham leaving the stage for twenty-seven verses, returning briefly to view silently the destruction. The focus of the first 26 verses in this chapter is on Lot and Sodom.

The two men accompanying the Lord at Abraham's tent are now identified as two angels. Only these two go on to Sodom. Lot, who is sitting at the gate, rises and bows when he sees them. He insists that they stay with him and he feeds them unleavened bread and "a feast." Before they lay down, the men of Sodom surround Lot's house and demand that the guests be sent out so they can "know" them. Lot begs the townspeople to leave the visitors alone and offers his two daughters instead. Lot is threatened, but he and his two daughters are saved by the angels who strike the men of the town blind. The angels ask Lot to gather his family and get ready to leave because they are going to destroy the city. In the morning, the angels tell Lot to leave immediately with his wife and two daughters. Lot does not comply and the angels drag him from the city. Lot is not allowed to flee to the hills but is permitted to go to the small nearby city of Zoar. After Lot's family reaches Zoar, Sodom and Gomorrah are destroyed by the raining down of sulfur and fire, killing all the inhabitants of the cities and the surrounding plain. Lot's wife is turned into a pillar of salt because she looked back, while Abraham silently views the destruction. The chapter ends with the seemingly odd and disconcerting story of Lot's daughters conspiring to get their father drunk and have sexual relations with him. We are told they bore him two sons, one the ancestor of the Moabites and the other the ancestor of the Ammonites.

There are sharp contrasts when we compare Abraham's greeting of the guests at his tent and Lot's greeting of the two guests at the city's gate. Abraham is portrayed in an altogether positive light.[3] Although Abraham is old, he runs to greet the visitors, and he makes a banquet using the best bread and the best food. Lot does not run to greet his guests, and he provides them unleavened bread and a feast that is not described. The implication in the lack of description is that Lot's greeting is something less than that of

Abraham.[4] There is an important nuance here: Abraham treats his guests in a better manner than Lot does.[5] This sets the stage for the demands made by the townspeople.

The odd story of Lot and his daughters' behavior in Zoar seems abhorrent to modern sensibilities. When the actions of Lot's daughters are taken with Lot's offering them to the townspeople of Sodom in place of the visiting angels, it makes the story even more incongruous. But there is another parallel occurring here, like the Abraham-Lot encounters with the visitors. In the chapter following the story of Lot, Abraham and Sarah enter as aliens into the region of Negeb. Abraham tells the king that Sarah is his sister and not his wife, and the king takes her away from him. God intercedes before the king has sex with Sarah, and she is restored to Abraham as his wife. At the beginning of the following chapter, Sarah conceives and bears Isaac. Abraham and Sarah are shown as upright and proper, made to appear even more so based on what had just transpired in the previous chapter between Lot and his daughters.

The sandwiching of the story of Lot and Sodom in the middle of the Abraham story allows the reader to more fully understand Abraham's journey of faith, highlights the way Abraham treats guests, and emphasizes God's keeping of the covenant promise made to Abraham.[6]

With that wider understanding of the passage, the Sodom and Gomorrah accounts takes on a different meaning. Genesis 19:4–5 says, "But before they lay down, the men of the city, the men of Sodom, both young and old, all the people to the last man, surrounded the house; and they called to Lot, 'Where are the men who came to you tonight? Bring them out to us, so that we may *know* them'" (emphasis added). Not all translations of this sentence utilize the word "know" to describe what the crowds of men are demanding. Others say (with emphasis added):

NASB: Bring them out to us that we may have *relations* with them.

NIV: Bring them out to us so that we can have *sex* with them.
The African American Jubilee Edition (CEV): Send them out, so we can have *sex* with them.
The Message/Remix: Bring them out so we can have our *sport* with them.

The Hebrew word that is utilized is in the imperfect tense, is in the first person common plural, is cohortive in both form and meaning, and is defined as: to know, to make known, to cause to know. The root of this Hebrew word refers to sexual relations. Based on Lot's reaction and his offering of his daughters who had not "known" a man, the implication of the word is that the men of the town were looking to have forced sexual relations with Lot's visitors: to gang rape them. The violence of the situation makes clear that the text is referring to multiple forced and violent sexual encounters. The translations other than the NRSV are not incorrect and appear to be attempting to make the text clearer in meaning and intent. But it is inaccurate to refer to the demands of the townspeople as "sex" or "sport," as rape is not sex in the mutual connotation of the word. Rape is violent assault.

Keeping in mind the wider story of Abraham, the account of Lot and Sodom performs the task of highlighting the differences between Abraham's generous and appropriate treatment of his guests as opposed to Sodom's. Although Lot himself was respectful to his guests, it is certainly not a response that our time and culture can understand.

> Lot's offer makes graphically clear the value of women relative to men. The practice of hospitality is a practice of men protecting men from men. Women are not protected, and women can be the means by which men are protected.[7]

Many commentators agree that the "sin" of Sodom is that the townspeople were guilty of the social sin of violent intent toward other human beings. The violent sexual act that the men were trying to perpetrate on the visitors is not the focus of the story.[8] Other commentators do not agree, claiming the focus on the inhospitable aspect of the men of Sodom is not the point but the attempted same-sex encounter is the major sin for which God punished Sodom.[9] The latter is a minority view expressed in commentaries.

The story of Sodom's destruction parallels another Genesis story and carries on a theme in Genesis. The Sodom saga parallels the story of the flood and God's promises to the patriarchs, the promise of descendents and God's covenant relationship. By juxtaposing these stories, Genesis is showing that divine judgment helps to provide humankind with another chance at redemption—at getting things right.[10]

This theme of God's judgment due to inappropriate activity on the part of humans is picked up throughout the writings in the Hebrew Testament and the Christian New Testament. The story of Sodom and Gomorrah is used numerous times as an example of what happens when God's people do not live up to God's expectations. It is important to note that none of these references to Sodom and Gomorrah in other biblical texts have to do with same-gender sexual activity.[11] These other verses have a common theme running through them: they involve a turning away from the proper worship of God. In Isaiah 1 and Jeremiah 23, as well as Deuteronomy 29, the prophets are lamenting Israel's turning away from God's law by worshiping false gods. In Amos 4, the prophet decries the treatment of the poor and the needy. In Zephaniah 2 and Ezekiel 16, the prophets warn Israel's enemies against pride and arrogance by their ignoring the poor and needy, and prophesy their destruction like Sodom and Gomorrah. The focus of all of these passages, and their references to what happened to Sodom and Gomorrah, is not on sex. These other biblical passages focus on a societal expectation that care and generosity be offered to widows, orphans, strangers, and the poor.

The Gospels of Matthew and Luke also refer to Sodom and Gomorrah. Each of these references occurs just after a rejection of Jesus by a people or town after he has finished teaching. These references to Sodom and Gomorrah by Jesus have nothing to do with sexual relations. Matthew 10 involves Jesus sending forth the disciples to do mission work but warns them that some will reject their teaching and that they should "shake off the dust from your feet" (verse 14). Jesus then prophesies that the town that rejects those disciples will be treated worse than Sodom and Gomorrah. In Matthew 11, Jesus castigates the cities that rejected both John the Baptist and Jesus's own teachings by saying on the Day of Judgment they will wish for the judgment that was delivered to Sodom and Gomorrah.

In Luke 10, the two Matthew stories are folded together into one sequence, with the same theme of rejection of Jesus and his disciples being the focus. Those who rejected Jesus and his disciples are told they will face punishment far worse than Sodom and Gomorrah. Luke 17 takes a slightly different approach in its reference to Sodom and Gomorrah. In this chapter Jesus heals ten lepers, but only one, a Samaritan, a foreigner, comes back to thank and worship Jesus. This event is immediately followed by the Pharisees asking Jesus when the kingdom of God is going to arrive. Jesus describes his coming as more terrible than the fate on Sodom and Gomorrah for those who did not believe and rejected him. Jesus's references to Sodom and Gomorrah are not focused on sexual conduct as the cause of the judgment.

Part Two: Judges 19

In those days, when there was no king in Israel, a certain
Levite, residing in the remote parts of the hill country of
Ephraim, took to himself a concubine from Bethlehem in
Judah. 2 But his concubine became angry with him, and she
went away from him to her father's house at Bethlehem in
Judah, and was there some four months. 3 Then her husband

set out after her, to speak tenderly to her and bring her back. He had with him his servant and a couple of donkeys. When he reached her father's house, the girl's father saw him and came with joy to meet him. 4 His father-in-law, the girl's father, made him stay, and he remained with him three days; so they ate and drank, and he stayed there. 5 On the fourth day they got up early in the morning, and he prepared to go; but the girl's father said to his son-in-law, "Fortify yourself with a bit of food, and after that you may go." 6 So the two men sat and ate and drank together; and the girl's father said to the man, "Why not spend the night and enjoy yourself?" 7 When the man got up to go, his father-in-law kept urging him until he spent the night there again. 8 On the fifth day he got up early in the morning to leave; and the girl's father said, "Fortify yourself." So they lingered until the day declined, and the two of them ate and drank. 9 When the man with his concubine and his servant got up to leave, his father-in-law, the girl's father, said to him, "Look, the day has worn on until it is almost evening. Spend the night. See, the day has drawn to a close. Spend the night here and enjoy yourself. Tomorrow you can get up early in the morning for your journey, and go home." 10 But the man would not spend the night; he got up and departed, and arrived opposite Jebus (that is, Jerusalem). He had with him a couple of saddled donkeys, and his concubine was with him. 11 When they were near Jebus, the day was far spent, and the servant said to his master, "Come now, let us turn aside to this city of the Jebusites, and spend the night in it." 12 But his master said to him, "We will not turn aside into a city of foreigners, who do not belong to the people of Israel; but we will continue on to Gibeah." 13 Then he said to his

servant, "Come, let us try to reach one of these places, and
spend the night at Gibeah or at Ramah." 14 So they passed on
and went their way; and the sun went down on them near
Gibeah, which belongs to Benjamin. 15 They turned aside
there, to go in and spend the night at Gibeah. He went in and
sat down in the open square of the city, but no one took them
in to spend the night. 16 Then at evening there was an old man
coming from his work in the field. The man was from the hill
country of Ephraim, and he was residing in Gibeah. (The
people of the place were Benjaminites.) 17 When the old man
looked up and saw the wayfarer in the open square of the city,
he said, "Where are you going and where do you come from?"
18 He answered him, "We are passing from Bethlehem in
Judah to the remote parts of the hill country of Ephraim, from
which I come. I went to Bethlehem in Judah; and I am going
to my home. Nobody has offered to take me in. 19 We your
servants have straw and fodder for our donkeys, with bread
and wine for me and the woman and the young man along
with us. We need nothing more." 20 The old man said, "Peace
be to you. I will care for all your wants; only do not spend the
night in the square." 21 So he brought him into his house, and
fed the donkeys; they washed their feet, and ate and drank.
22 While they were enjoying themselves, the men of the city,
a perverse lot, surrounded the house, and started pounding
on the door. They said to the old man, the master of the house,
"Bring out the man who came into your house, so that we may
have intercourse with him." 23 And the man, the master of the
house, went out to them and said to them, "No, my brothers,
do not act so wickedly. Since this man is my guest, do not do
this vile thing. 24 Here are my virgin daughter and his concubine;

let me bring them out now. Ravish them and do whatever
you want to them; but against this man do not do such a vile
thing." [25] But the men would not listen to him. So the man
seized his concubine, and put her out to them. They wantonly
raped her, and abused her all through the night until the
morning. And as the dawn began to break, they let her go.
[26] As morning appeared, the woman came and fell down at
the door of the man's house where her master was, until it was
light. [27] In the morning her master got up, opened the doors of
the house, and when he went out to go on his way, there was
his concubine lying at the door of the house, with her hands
on the threshold. [28] "Get up," he said to her, "we are going."
But there was no answer. Then he put her on the donkey;
and the man set out for his home. [29] When he had entered his
house, he took a knife, and grasping his concubine he cut her
into twelve pieces, limb by limb, and sent her throughout all
the territory of Israel. [30] Then he commanded the men whom
he sent, saying, "Thus shall you say to all the Israelites, 'Has
such a thing ever happened since the day that the Israelites
came up from the land of Egypt until this day? Consider it,
take counsel, and speak out.'"

The book of Judges chronicles Israel's quest to possess the Promised Land of Canaan that was designated as theirs in Genesis. Judges 19 is toward the end of the accounts. In some ways it is a pivotal story in the book, just as Judges can be seen as the pivotal book in this cycle of writings in the Hebrew Testament. Judges sets the background necessary to appreciate the story for the royal rulers to come in succeeding books. Unsurprisingly, similar themes as seen in Genesis play an important part in chapter

19 of Judges and are an integral part in deciphering the nuances in the chapter. Before this chapter is looked at in detail, a review of general principles found in Judges will provide a better understanding. It is a collection of stories about different local leaders from disparate Jewish communities. Israel had no overarching monarch at this time, but was ruled by local city-state rulers and civil administrators. These individuals become inspired by God's Word and lead local Israelite tribes against their enemies.[12]

All of the stories preceding chapter 19 illustrate a steady downward spiral of Israel and its leaders, culminating in the horrendous acts of the unnamed Levite and members of the Benjaminite tribe of Israel.[13] The stories in Judges show an escalating series of events that highlight growing anarchy and a reckless disregard for traditions, laws, and customs by the tribes of Israel.[14] The series of stories before chapter 19 demonstrate how the inappropriate actions of the tribes of Israel, each worse than the last, lead to a lessening of their ability to hold on to Israel's Promised Land. These scenes of increasing anarchy appear with the repeated refrain, "In those days, when there was no king in Israel."[15] Much of what happens in Judges provides the basis for what comes in the succeeding biblical books: the need for the establishment of a royal line of leaders in Israel. These stories in Judges are circular in nature, similar but each succeeding one showcasing worse behavior and a spiraling downward of societal norms and behaviors. Upon reaching chapter 19, a crisis of leadership is clearly found, or more accurately the lack of leadership is clearly acknowledged.[16] Judges plainly points out that the successes and failures of Israel are connected to Israel's faithfulness or unfaithfulness to God's covenants. Nonetheless God graciously and continuously intervenes to assist the people.[17]

Throughout the book of Judges, Israel's decline is reflected in the treatment of women. The health and faithfulness of Israel is in far better shape at the beginning of the book of Judges, where women are treated fairly and are shown to have independence.

At the end of the book, as exemplified in chapter 19 and the following chapters, women are treated abysmally: they are treated as objects, possessions, and nonpersons, with a corresponding unhealthiness reflected in Israel's fortunes and actions.[18]

Chapter 19 is the beginning of the conclusion of Judges. It sets the stage for the tale of an Israelite civil war, with the rape of the Levite's concubine being the catalyst.[19] Women and their treatment in this book of the Hebrew Testament, as well as the actions and misdeeds of the unnamed Levite, provide fertile ground for the growth of the monarchy in the following books.

Judges chronicles Israel's inability to defeat its enemies because of their lack of faithfulness to God. The narrative structure created by the authors of Judges largely frames this theological idea: linking faithfulness to God's teachings to their success against enemies.[20] There is a repeated rhetorical framework in most of the stories in the book of Judges: Israel does evil, and they have trouble with oppressors. Israel cries to God for help, and God sends a deliverer who defeats the oppressor. Then there is relative peace while the judge still lives. As the stories proceed, this cycle begins to break down until we get to chapter 19, where it is completely defunct.[21] It is a subtle chapter. If it is read in too cursory a fashion, these subtleties and nuances can easily be missed.

The authors of Judges use irony quite frequently and in particular in chapter 19. God had appointed the Levites (as one of the twelve tribes of Israel) to teach the Israelites to observe the law God handed to them.[22] It is ironic that the main character in chapter 19 should be "a certain Levite," who himself has been described as perhaps the most despicable character in the book of Judges.[23] By focusing on the Levites, chapter 19 is condemning all of Israel by exhibiting the extent of society's moral decline: depravity has reached even those who were charged by God with being the teachers and models of the law.[24]

Chapter 19 begins with a concubine leaving her husband. It is unclear why the Levite's concubine left. Differing translations offer differing clues, some charging her with adultery, others saying she was unfaithful. The simple act of leaving her husband would constitute unfaithfulness under Jewish law. The fact that the husband chases after her to bring her home makes adultery seem a farfetched explanation of her departure. The reader gets a hint that something is not right when this Levite goes to his father-in-law's house "to speak tenderly to her" (19:3). This seemingly innocuous phrase should strike fear in the heart of the reader because this exact phrase was used in Genesis by another ignoble character: Shechem. He used this phrase when he was trying to woo Dinah into marrying him, even though he had already raped her.[25] The authors of Judges are foreshadowing for the reader that all is not right with this Levite, and his concubine is in danger.

Another literary feature of this passage is quite beautiful and heartbreaking. After the Levite's concubine is gang raped all night long, she struggles to the door behind which her husband is sleeping and collapses there with "her hands on the threshold" (19:27). She is grasping the threshold of where she was supposed to have safe haven and protection, but had received none. The threshold and her grasping at it are metaphors for what has been lost in Israel. She was shown no safety and will continue to be abused, contrary to all the laws concerning obligations and duties to family. The threshold, representative of God's laws, holds no place of sanctuary for her any longer.[26]

What occurs in chapter 19 of Judges is horrific. The actions of the people of Gibeah are a foreshadowing of what comes after the story. The resulting civil war does not correct the problem; instead that war leads to worse acts committed against countless other female victims, compounding the original offense as opposed to avenging it.[27] The book of Judges ends in a very grim fashion, leaving the Israelite people behaving in any manner they please in violation of God's law: a metaphor for Israel being lost without a king.[28] The horrific acts in chapter 19 exemplify how

Israel lost its understanding of what it means to follow God, and what it means to be committed to family and community. This ultimately is part of the explanation of Israel's losing the Promised Land that God had gifted to them.[29]

Chapter 19 has strong parallels to the Genesis story of Abraham and Lot and the town of Sodom. Yet there are important differences, making the Judges story a far worse one; for ultimately in Sodom the visitors or daughters were not raped, while in Gibeah the concubine was gang raped.[30] In Judges, the visitors this time are not angels, but a Levite and his concubine. Upon entering the city of Gibeah, a city populated by the Israelite tribe of Benjamin, the visitors are ignored by its residents, unlike Lot who met the angels and welcomed them at the gate. This development is a further piece of irony provided to us by the authors of Judges. The Levite had deliberately avoided going into non-Israelite towns for fear of not being treated appropriately. They did not receive appropriate treatment in Gibeah. A further irony is that an individual from the tribe of Levi was supposed to have been treated with even more respect than a common stranger, as he was a teacher of the law.[31] In Exodus, Leviticus, and Deuteronomy, the writings are clear that all of Israel is to be generously hospitable to the stranger, commanding that Israel remember that they were once strangers in Egypt.[32] Gibeah's lack of response is an example of how far away the people of Israel have moved from God's teachings.

The parallels between the accounts in Judges and Genesis are further illustrated by contrasting how the Levite was treated upon arrival at the family home of his concubine as against the saga of Abraham. The exaggerated welcome the Levite's father-in-law showered on him and the favor shown the Levite by the foreigner in Gibeah parallels that of the story of Abraham's hospitality to God and the angels, and Lot's hospitality to the angels in Sodom. Although not exactly alike, these two stories mirror each other. The parallels continue with the men who arrive pounding on the door seeking to rape the visitors. From this point forward, the parallels cease. In Sodom, God intervenes and strikes the aggressors blind, thereby sparing the angels and Lot's daughters. In Gibeah, there is no intervention from God. The Levite's foreigner host offers his own virgin daughter and his guest's concubine as substitute for the Levite. This is not satisfactory to the Benjaminites in Gibeah, and apparently in a panic the Levite strong-arms his concubine out the door, where the aggressors transgress in ways the men of Sodom were prevented by their blindness.

There are other disconnections between the Genesis story and Judges 19. Chief among these disconnections is that the rapists in Gibeah are members of the Israelite family of tribes. They are Benjaminites as opposed to people outside of the Israelite nation as in the Sodom story. A further disconnect that indicates the debasement of Israel is the apathy of the Levite himself. After having pushed his concubine out to be raped and tortured, he apparently goes to sleep unperturbed. Upon arising in the morning. he shows no concern for her, telling her to get up from the door's threshold as he is ready to leave. The reader is left uncertain if she is dead or alive, up to and including the point where the Levite dismembers her into twelve pieces to be grotesquely paraded around Israel.[33]

The importance of the Gibeahean crowd's insistence on raping the Levite is a point of contention among commentators. Some barely make a mention of it, simply citing a mirrored parallelism to the Sodom story and focusing on the abuse of the concubine by not only the men of the town but by her husband and their host.[34] Both Allish Eves and Sharon Niditch go into more detail about the significance of the attempted rape of the Levite. Eves says that both the Levite and his host viewed the rape of a male as being the worse of two evils, as it involved "a sexual connection abominated in Israelite culture and religion."[35] Niditch claims that ancient Israelites viewed the rape of a male as antisocial behavior equivalent to cannibalism in the Greek culture. She goes on to say that the Benjaminites threat of rape of the Levite signals that they are "consummately aggressive, prepared to act out in a literal way which is the metaphor of conquest in war."[36]

Judges was written in the time period of the eighth to the seventh centuries BCE. This was a time of social and political upheavals, both internally and externally, with both the Northern Kingdom and the Southern Kingdom of Israel facing military threats from Assyria, the neighboring superpower.[37] Judges chronicles a period in Israel's history having taken place approximately 500 years earlier than its writing and spanning a time period of approximately 200 years in duration.[38] The purpose behind Judges was to provide some explanation for why God would leave Israel in such difficult political and social conditions as it found itself. One of the things that Judges does is to indicate what happens to people and communities when they lack good moral leaders who follow God's ordinances.[39]

The original audience would have discerned a condemnation of King Saul, who was deposed by David. Saul was from Gibeah and the tribe of Benjamin. The early audience would have drawn a connection to the treatment of the Levite in Saul's hometown and seen a condemnation of Saul himself and of his reign. The early audience would see the text as claiming Saul's rule was besmirched by the actions of his ancestors: in other words, the story in chapter 19 is character assassination of an overthrown leader.[40]

The early audience of Judges would have seen that the attack on the Levite and his concubine as an assault, not by a foreigner or against a foreigner, but by and against members of the Israelite family. These initial audience would have been drawn to a conclusion that the twelve tribes of Israel were disintegrating.[41] It is highly unlikely that the initial audience would have viewed this text as a polemic against queer people.

Part Three: Discussion

Neither of these two passages is focused on "homosexuality." Neither are these stories about sex; they are about rape. Rape is a deliberate act of violence and an abuse of power. Rape has nothing to do with sex, whether it is male-on-male or male-on-female. This violation of another human has to do with power and violence, and the sin of the intentional degradation of another person. Both of these stories focus on the wrongful and sinful taking of another person's dignity in a sinfully violent act of humiliation.

To understand what the original authors' intentions were in the Genesis and Judges stories, certain modern preconceptions of sex, and masculinity and femininity, need to be modified. In the times when these texts were developed and passed down from generation to generation, distinctions were not drawn between homosexual and heterosexual but between free and slave, dominant and subordinate, strong and weak. The alignment of male and female or male and male was not in the gender construction/orientation of relationships. The alignment was about power in those relationships.[42]

The understanding at that time was that a person who was used sexually by another person was weaker than the aggressor.[43] Many sexual acts were about dominance of the stronger against the weaker, the superior against the inferior, no matter the gender of the weaker, inferior individual.[44] This attitude makes clearer the actions of the Benjaminites in Gibeah. Although they demanded that the Levite be brought out so they could rape him, they accepted his concubine as a substitute. It did not matter which one they raped, it was all about power. They wanted to debase and degrade the Levite. By raping his concubine, a member of his family for whom he was responsible, they were also degrading him. These stories are all about power, who has it, and how that power is utilized. They are not exemplars of God's dislike or bias against queer people.

These stories of the near rape in Genesis and the gang rape in Judges assist in the understanding of how society should not act in Hebrew Testament days. The following Hebrew Testament passages also provide guidelines for appropriate societal conduct:

Exodus 22:21: You shall not wrong or oppress a resident alien, for you were aliens in the land of Egypt.
Exodus 23:9: You shall not oppress a resident alien; you know the heart of an alien, for you were aliens in the land of Egypt.
Leviticus 19:33–34: When an alien resides with you in your land, you shall not oppress the alien. [34] The alien who resides with you shall be to you as the citizen among you; you shall love the alien as yourself, for you were aliens in the land of Egypt: I am the LORD your God.
Deuteronomy 10:18 –19: Who executes justice for the orphan and the widow, and who loves the strangers, providing them food and clothing. [19] You shall also love the stranger, for you were strangers in the land of Egypt.
Deuteronomy 16:14: Rejoice during your festival, you and your sons and your daughters, your male and female slaves, as well as the Levites, the strangers, the orphans, and the widows resident in your towns.
Deuteronomy 26:12: When you have finished paying all the tithe of your produce in the third year (which is the year of the tithe), giving it to the Levites, the aliens, the orphans, and the widows, so that they may eat their fill within your towns,

God wants us to love the stranger, the alien, the foreigner. This theme is carried forward into the Christian New Testament with Jesus defining the greatest commandment: "'You shall love the Lord your God with all your heart, and with all your soul, and with all your mind.' This is the greatest and first commandment. And a second is like it: 'You shall love your neighbor as yourself.'"[45] Both the Hebrew Testament and the Christian Testament are clear that how we act as a society ranks second only to loving God. When those God-centric values are violated, society collapses.

Genesis 19 and Judges 19 are about living into God's covenant through the lens of the negative storyline of how not to live into righteousness and justice. The two chapters are focused on examples of humans not living into God's covenant but who instead are degrading others. They are not about mutual sexual relations among queer people, but are about the inappropriate activity on the part of humans in the wrongful taking, the rape of another person. They focus on power, and the abuse of that power.

CHAPTER TWO

Leviticus 18 and 20

Part One: Leviticus 18

The LORD spoke to Moses, saying: 2 Speak to the people of Israel and say to them: I am the LORD your God. 3 You shall not do as they do in the land of Egypt, where you lived, and you shall not do as they do in the land of Canaan, to which I am bringing you. You shall not follow their statutes. 4 My ordinances you shall observe and my statutes you shall keep, following them: I am the LORD your God. 5 You shall keep my statutes and my ordinances; by doing so one shall live: I am the LORD. 6 None of you shall approach anyone near of kin to uncover nakedness: I am the LORD. 7 You shall not uncover the nakedness of your father, which is the nakedness of your mother; she is your mother, you shall not uncover her nakedness. 8 You shall not uncover the nakedness of your father's wife; it is the nakedness of your father. 9 You shall not uncover the nakedness of your sister, your father's daughter or your mother's daughter, whether born at home or born abroad. 10 You shall not uncover the nakedness of your son's daughter or of your daughter's daughter, for their nakedness is your own

nakedness. [11] You shall not uncover the nakedness of your
father's wife's daughter, begotten by your father, since she
is your sister. [12] You shall not uncover the nakedness of your
father's sister; she is your father's flesh. [13] You shall not
uncover the nakedness of your mother's sister, for she is your
mother's flesh. [14] You shall not uncover the nakedness of your
father's brother, that is, you shall not approach his wife; she
is your aunt. [15] You shall not uncover the nakedness of your
daughter-in-law: she is your son's wife; you shall not uncover
her nakedness. [16] You shall not uncover the nakedness of your
brother's wife; it is your brother's nakedness. [17] You shall not
uncover the nakedness of a woman and her daughter, and you
shall not take her son's daughter or her daughter's daughter
to uncover her nakedness; they are your flesh; it is depravity.
[18] And you shall not take a woman as a rival to her sister,
uncovering her nakedness while her sister is still alive. [19] You
shall not approach a woman to uncover her nakedness while
she is in her menstrual uncleanness. [20] You shall not have
sexual relations with your kinsman's wife, and defile yourself
with her. [21] You shall not give any of your offspring to sacrifice
them to Molech, and so profane the name of your God: I am
the LORD. [22] You shall not lie with a male as with a woman; it
is an abomination. [23] You shall not have sexual relations with
any animal and defile yourself with it, nor shall any woman
give herself to an animal to have sexual relations with it: it
is perversion. [24] Do not defile yourselves in any of these ways,
for by all these practices the nations I am casting out before
you have defiled themselves. [25] Thus the land became defiled;
and I punished it for its iniquity, and the land vomited out
its inhabitants. [26] But you shall keep my statutes and my

ordinances and commit none of these abominations, either the
citizen or the alien who resides among you [27] (for the inhabitants of the land, who were before you, committed all of these
abominations, and the land became defiled); [28] otherwise the
land will vomit you out for defiling it, as it vomited out the
nation that was before you. [29] For whoever commits any of
these abominations shall be cut off from their people. [30] So
keep my charge not to commit any of these abominations that
were done before you, and not to defile yourselves by them:
I am the LORD your God.

Leviticus is a difficult book to comprehend, much misunderstood and often incorrectly interpreted and utilized. Over the course of time, many traditions and commentators have mistakenly ignored it. To begin to understand Leviticus 18:22 we need a broader view of the book.

Leviticus is the third book of the Bible, placed between Exodus and Numbers. Exodus is the long story of Israel's escape from captivity in Egypt and their journey of faith wandering in the desert while trying to figure out, unsuccessfully, how actually to be God's chosen people.[1] Numbers, which follows Leviticus, chronicles events during the people's travels and adventures in the wilderness interspersed with behavioral rules and obligations. Numbers concludes with the preparation for the end of the people's wanderings and their entrance into the Promised Land.

The five books of the Pentateuch, or Torah—Genesis, Exodus, Leviticus, Numbers, and Deuteronomy—have been called the "Books of Moses" with ancient tradition claiming they were written by him. More recent scholarship provides a different interpretation. Whether the Pentateuch is a collection of documents written from the ninth to the fifth centuries, BCE, as propounded by Wellhausen, or books that represent the strong oral traditions of that time used to supplement the shorter written documents until the oral traditions were compiled into one set of five books during Israel's exile (Gunkel), Leviticus appears to always have been a part of this important set of books for the people of Israel.[2]

There are legal materials in Exodus as well as in Numbers, instructing the people of Israel in the ways to act, how to stay a separate people, and in how to deepen their relationship with God. Leviticus serves as a link between Exodus and Numbers, tying them together.[3] Commentators argue that Leviticus cannot be ignored, as it is so often, but rather must be considered the very center of the Pentateuch, which is the very heart of the Hebrew Bible.[4] Interpreters should not jury-pick certain sections and passages without explaining how those sections fit into the whole of the chapter, the whole of the book, and as one piece of the larger Pentateuch.

The predominant topic in the book of Leviticus is holiness: holiness of the people, holiness of actions and rituals, holiness of relationships, and holiness in relationship to God.[5] Leviticus can be broadly divided into two sections: chapters 1–16 are instructions to priests, while chapters 17–27 are instructions from priests to the people of Israel.[6] A more detailed breakdown of Leviticus's structure takes those two broad sections and divides them into:

Chapters 1–7 as the regulations in regard to sacrifices;
Chapters 8–10 as the initiation into appropriate worship rituals;
Chapters 11–15 as the purification and purity codes;
Chapter 16 as establishing the Yom Kippur (the atonement) festival;
Chapters 17–26 as establishing the "Holiness Code" for the general public; and
Chapter 27 as establishing vows and dedications.[7]

The priestly section, chapters 1–16, is for the most part written in a legalistic and impersonal style. The presentation of the material in chapters 17–26, where the "Holiness Code" for the people of Israel is set forth, is distinctly different from the first section. In this broad second half of Leviticus, God, through the priests, is speaking directly to the chosen people. These latter chapters of Leviticus utilize "I" and "you," which provide a framework for demands and commands for the people to follow.[8] This is further evidence of the shift in focus of Leviticus from one broad section of how to be a priest, to the next: from instructions to priests, to instructions from the priests to the people.

Leviticus 18 falls into the "Holiness Code." The term "holiness" draws the focus of the reader and provides instruction in how to worship God. Part of the underlying theological principles of that worship is an understanding in Leviticus of the "yawning gulf between the character of God and the character [of human beings]," and to assist in the understanding that God is utterly different from us.[9] The broad first section of Leviticus focuses on holiness in the sphere of the tabernacle, where God is believed present, and what the requisite actions of the priest are to worship in that sacred place. Chapter 18 focuses on a spreading of this holiness out from the temple to include the whole world.[10] The Holiness Code provides instructions to Israel on how to be holy in almost all areas of life, in all their actions. This was intended to instill in the people an understanding that holiness is a way and manner of life. It is not just following one set of rules.[11]

The laws and rules set forth in chapter 18 of Leviticus can be broken into two broad categories of forbidden relationships: incest and other forbidden sexual encounters.[12] In the first category, found in 18:6–18, sexual relationships that are taboo while a wife is alive are with: mother, stepmother, full sister or half sister, granddaughter, stepsister, paternal aunt, maternal aunt, paternal uncle's wife, daughter-in-law, sister-in-law, stepdaughter of the man, and a wife's sister. The other forbidden encounters are found in 18:19–23: sex with someone menstruating, adultery, (offspring being sacrificed to Molech,) male/male encounters (v. 22), and bestiality.[13] The phrase "I am the Lord your God" appears five times in this chapter and serves as brackets around the different sections and brings a ring of authority to those statements.[14]

Before we dive into a review of the various prohibited conducts and how they impact verse 22, it should be noted that at both the beginning and the end of chapter 18, the text makes an interesting use of the land as an image, bracketing as seen in Genesis. God warns the people not to act like the Canaanites, who are about to be supplanted when Israel is granted the land by God. The author(s) of Leviticus are setting the people of Israel apart from those societies around them. Conduct judged to be immoral is not only considered to be a defilement of the person involved in that conduct, but is also a defilement of the land itself. Sacrifice and loss of the land will be the result should the conduct that takes place in the land be judged immoral.[15] The land that is about to be gifted to them by God and the life of the people of Israel are intrinsically woven together by these references.[16] Should the people not follow these rules and regulations, they will not be holy. A consequence of not being holy will be loss of the land. It is important to remember that these works were written and edited when that land had already been lost and the people of Israel were in exile, seeking an understanding for that banishment.

In the first series of prohibited behaviors set forth in 18:6–18, the phrase "uncover the nakedness of" is utilized to describe the behavior being discouraged. The phrase is a euphemism for sexual intercourse.[17] This euphemism stems from the idea that the husband and wife are one flesh (Gen. 2:24). To "uncover the nakedness" of one is equivalent to uncovering the nakedness of the other: married partners are considered "one flesh."[18] Although these rules against incest existed, a loophole also existed for first cousins to marry.[19] Some argue that this is a fitting loophole, as the Israelite community was a closed society. This allowance limited the need to go outside the Israelite community to arrange a marriage, allowing the closed society to propagate.[20]

The phrase "uncover the nakedness of" appears for the first time in the Torah in Genesis 9:20–27 and the story of Noah. Ham, the father of Canaan, "saw the nakedness of" Noah who had collapsed drunk in his tent. Ham laughingly told his brothers Shem and Japheth, and they in turn walked into the tent backwards and covered their father with a blanket. There have been several differing opinions rendered as to what Ham did and saw in the tent of his father from which no real consensus has been reached. Some type of transgression obviously took place because of Noah's reaction upon awakening from his drunken stupor, but the gravity of the act perpetrated upon him is not known. There is no definitive rabbinic interpretation of this pericope, these interpretations range from Ham tying a rope around Noah's genitals and trying to castrate him, to Ham raping Noah, to Ham demeaning his elderly father and being disrespectful of him to and in front of his brothers.[21]

Brueggemann argues that the transgressions against Noah were more symbolic. "It may mean to penetrate the ultimate personal mystery of the parents by probing their most vulnerable action or condition."[22] The shame of Ham has to do with something similar to the forbidden fruit from the tree of knowledge in the Garden of Eden. It is a prohibition that reflects some type of sexual agenda and is concerned with the mystery of life and procreation.[23] Interestingly, the story does not dwell on Ham's offense but focuses instead on the political results of that action: the subjugation of Ham's descendents, the Canaanites. This story of Noah and Ham sets forth a rationale to explain and justify, on theological grounds, the power relationship between Israel and Canaan by later redactors of the story.[24]

The second grouping of prohibited conduct in Leviticus chapter 18 is set forth in verses 19–23 and represents a different kind of prohibition.

Verse 19: you shall not uncover the nakedness of woman during her menstruation
Verse 20: you shall not have sexual relations with a kinsman's wife
Verse 21: you shall not give your offspring as a sacrifice to Molech
Verse 22: you shall not lie with a male as with a woman
Verse 23: you shall not have sexual relations with an animal nor shall a woman have sexual relations with an animal

These prohibitions are nonfamilial in nature, with two exceptions, verse 20 (no sex with a kinsman's wife) and verse 21 (the prohibition against the giving of offspring for sacrifice to Molech).

Verse 22, as translated above, uses the phrase "lie with" to describe the prohibited conduct. This phrase is in the second person imperfect conjugation in Hebrew. The Hebrew words utilized are *mishkab* and *shakab*. *Shakab* can be translated as "to lay with," while *mishkab* is often translated as lie in the lying place."[25] This is the only time in the Bible that these two Hebrew words are used together. The literal translation of verse 22 can be rendered: "With a male you are not to lie (after the manner of) lying with a woman, it is an abomination!"[26]

These two Hebrew words, *mishkab* and *shakab*, also differ from words utilized in regard to other descriptions of sexual conduct in Leviticus. *Shakab*, to lie with, is utilized numerous times in the Bible. Some examples are:

Leviticus 15:20: Everything upon which she lies during her impurity shall be unclean; everything also upon which she sits shall be unclean.

Leviticus 15:26: Every bed on which she lies during all the days of her discharge shall be treated as the bed of her impurity;

and everything on which she sits shall be unclean, as in the uncleanness of her impurity.

Leviticus 18:22: You shall not lie with a male as with a woman; it is an abomination.

Deuteronomy 24:12: If the person is poor, you shall not sleep in the garment given you as the pledge.

2 Samuel 12:3: but the poor man had nothing but one little ewe lamb, which he had bought. He brought it up, and it grew up with him and with his children; it used to eat of his meager fare, and drink from his cup, and lie in his bosom, and it was like a daughter to him.

Job 11:18: And you will have confidence, because there is hope; you will be protected and take your rest in safety.

Job 20:11: Their bodies, once full of youth, will lie down in the dust with them.

Proverbs 3:24: If you sit down, you will not be afraid; when you lie down, your sleep will be sweet.

Proverbs 6:9: How long will you lie there, O lazybones? When will you rise from your sleep?

Ezekiel 4:4: Then lie on your left side, and place the punishment of the house of Israel upon it; you shall bear their punishment for the number of the days that you lie there.

Ezekiel 31:18: Which among the trees of Eden was like you in glory and in greatness? Now you shall be brought down with the trees of Eden to the world below; you shall lie among the uncircumcised, with those who are killed by the sword. This is Pharaoh and all his horde, says the Lord God.

Jeremiah 3:24–25: "But from our youth the shameful thing has devoured all for which our ancestors had labored, their flocks and their herds, their sons and their daughters. Let us lie down in our shame, and let our dishonor cover us; for we have sinned against the Lord our God, we and our ancestors, from our youth even to this day; and we have not obeyed the voice of the Lord our God."

In the nine places in the Bible in which the Hebrew word *mishkab* is utilized, seven of those times that word is translated either as bed or couch or act of lying down.[27] Hebrew is a reflective language where the reflection goes from the verb to the noun. Here the word is meant to provide an inflection, to give a tone and understanding to the word to which it is providing depth. Using this word is a way to enhance the metaphorical quality of language, thereby yielding nuance and beauty and subtle meaning.

Mishkab, literally "in the place of lying," the untranslated word, is providing enhanced meaning to *shakab*, "to lie down." Another way to translate the verse is "to lie down in the place of lying a male shall not as with a woman."[28] All but one of the twelve incidents above provides a tinge of humiliation—of shame—to the "lying down." To lie down is to do something that is inappropriate, to act in a manner that is out of character for the culture of that time. For a man to act as a woman, "lying down in the place of lying" as a woman, to act in a manner that did not keep the power-center in the man, would be shameful. This action would be humiliation not only upon the man, but on society and how power was structured and understood. This type of action would be challenging the patriarchal system that existed in that society and culture.

Some argue that the prohibition in Leviticus 18:22 of a man "lying with another man as with a woman" reflects the belief that God created individuals for procreation, as in Genesis 1:26–28, where the instruction is given for humans to be fruitful and multiply. Leviticus 18:22 reflects this understanding that sexual activity is only for that stated purpose.[29] The Roman Catholic Church argues that Leviticus "is not just a formal set of laws; it provides moral rules which contain teachings about God and about man, and about man's relationship with God."[30]

The growth in the number of people within the Israelite family unit was crucial to the survival of Israel. Some commentators argue that this is one of the chief reasons for these rules about sex and sexuality: the survival of the nation of Israel was at stake if it did not reproduce in appropriate numbers.[31]

Other commentators take this argument one step further, saying Leviticus sets up a rigid code about how God created the world based on the understanding of the Levitical priest cult. In their worldview, God created the world from chaos: created the animals, and set human beings over all that was created. Human beings are to be fruitful and to multiply, and for a man to lie with a man as with a woman is to "sow a seed where it cannot grow and produce its fruit."[32] These same commentators argue that the priests who created Leviticus believed that there are categories of creation. Within those categories, human beings must conform to the class to which they have been assigned, thereby causing no confusion. For a man to be treated as a woman would cause confusion and is therefore prohibited.[33] By acting in this prohibited way, the foundations of society would be threatened by undermining the social structures that the book of Leviticus tried to put in place.[34]

Verse 22 falls into the "other prohibitions" portion of chapter 18, along with the sacrifice of children to Molech and bestiality. The land that the people of Israel were about to enter and take control of, as well as the Egyptian land they had left decades earlier, had pagan worship rituals that involved these sexual and sacrificial practices,[35] which would have been viewed by the priests as not acceptable to their worldview of why Israel was created. The priestly writers wanted to keep the people of Israel separate and distinct from the cultures surrounding them. These cultures surrounding the Israelite people were sensate societies lauding the unrestrained sexual practices of their gods that were emulated by the people who worshiped them.[36] The idea of separateness from other nations is critical to the understanding of what is in Leviticus: separateness based on their obedience to these rules; separateness based on their story of exodus from Egypt; separateness based on their fundamental belief that God set them apart; and the belief that God chose them from among all other people to be special and distinct.[37]

The rules and regulations in Leviticus provide clues to the kind of society for which it was written.[38] Leviticus was written by and for a patriarchal-centered society, treating women as something less then their male counterparts, peripheral to society, as well as a threat to the purity of the priesthood cult.[39] This andocentric mentality and the cultural and societal need to increase the population base of God's chosen people led the priestly authors of Leviticus to want to control women's bodies and their reproductive capabilities, and to protect "the seed" that sexual intercourse implants, thereby increasing procreation.[40]

As we have seen, Leviticus is focused on both the responsibilities of priests and how they are to teach the public appropriate ways to act, think, and understand the world around them. Women are treated as less than second-class citizens in the book; their normal bodily functions are presented in a degrading fashion and as something unclean.[41] In ancient Israel a woman was legally owned and was the property first of her father and then of her husband. A woman had few to no legal rights of her own. This understanding is buttressed by the observation that a woman's perspective is not incorporated into the text of the laws in Leviticus.[42] Although the rules in Leviticus are from a male point of view, the Levitical priests who wrote these laws intended them to prepare, teach, and train the people of Israel to be shining examples of God's presence in the world, and to set them apart from the world that surrounded them.[43] The male-centeredness, the distinct quality with which the Israelite community was to be imbued, and the lack of any standing of women are all critical concepts to keep in mind when reading Leviticus.

These laws and rules place emphasis on the belief that God is holy, different, and distant. Yet God resides among the people, making it necessary for them to be holy. The holiness of the people was a mark of distinction, allowing them to be separate and distinct from the surrounding cultures and societies.[44] Leviticus marks a specific way the people can be in relationship with God, the God who promised to be with them, among them, and provide a land for them. The Levitical priests were attempting to instill holiness, as they understood it, into every aspect of the people's lives.[45]

To "lie with a male as with a woman" is described as an "abomination." The *Merriam-Webster Dictionary* defines abomination as "something abominable, having extreme disgust and hatred for, having loathing for." "Abominable" is defined in the same dictionary as "detestable, something that is quite disagreeable or unpleasant." The root of the word "abomination" is defined as to hate or to abhor.[46]

The word "abomination" in its singular or plural forms is used 119 times in the Bible. Of its ten appearances in Leviticus, seven of those are in chapter 18 or 20. Two of those seven appearances are in the verses under our consideration. The five other times where the word is utilized in chapters 18 and 20, the authors use the word to explain that God is warning the people to keep the ordinances promulgated in Leviticus and not do any of the proscribed acts which are generally called "abomination(s)."[47] Those proscribed acts are varied. Leviticus 20:25 warns the people to keep clean and unclean animals and clean and unclean birds separate, for to mix them would be abomination. The three other uses of the word "abomination" in Leviticus forbid the eating of the flesh of the sacrifice on the third day (Leviticus 7:8 and 19:7) and forbid the eating of eagles, vultures, and osprey, as they are abominations (Leviticus 7:8).

The utilization of the word "abomination" in describing the conduct of a male lying with a male as with a female, and of the eating of an unclean animal, such as an eagle, vulture, or osprey, leads to a conclusion that lying with a male as with a female is different from "uncovering the nakedness" of a family member. "Uncovering the nakedness" of a family member is interpreted as having sexual relations with that individual, but is not considered "abomination." The use of the words "lying with" and "abomination" regarding male on male activity indicates those kinds of actions and conduct were thought of as something different than sexual relations. This will be explored further following a review of the next reference.

Part Two: Leviticus 20

The Lord spoke to Moses, saying: 2 Say further to the people
of Israel: Any of the people of Israel, or of the aliens who
reside in Israel, who give any of their offspring to Molech
shall be put to death; the people of the land shall stone them
to death. 3 I myself will set my face against them, and will
cut them off from the people, because they have given of their
offspring to Molech, defiling my sanctuary and profaning
my holy name. 4 And if the people of the land should ever
close their eyes to them, when they give of their offspring to
Molech, and do not put them to death, 5 I myself will set my
face against them and against their family, and will cut them
off from among their people, them and all who follow them
in prostituting themselves to Molech. 6 If any turn to mediums
and wizards, prostituting themselves to them, I will set my
face against them, and will cut them off from the people.
7 Consecrate yourselves therefore, and be holy; for I am the
Lord your God. 8 Keep my statutes, and observe them; I am
the Lord; I sanctify you. 9 All who curse father or mother
shall be put to death; having cursed father or mother, their
blood is upon them. 10 If a man commits adultery with the

wife of his neighbor, both the adulterer and the adulteress
shall be put to death. [11] The man who lies with his father's
wife has uncovered his father's nakedness; both of them shall
be put to death; their blood is upon them. [12] If a man lies with
his daughter-in-law, both of them shall be put to death; they
have committed perversion, their blood is upon them. [13] If
a man lies with a male as with a woman, both of them have
committed an abomination; they shall be put to death; their
blood is upon them. [14] If a man takes a wife and her mother
also, it is depravity; they shall be burned to death, both he
and they, that there may be no depravity among you. [15] If a
man has sexual relations with an animal, he shall be put to
death; and you shall kill the animal. [16] If a woman approaches
any animal and has sexual relations with it, you shall kill the
woman and the animal; they shall be put to death, their blood
is upon them. [17] If a man takes his sister, a daughter of his
father or a daughter of his mother, and sees her nakedness,
and she sees his nakedness, it is a disgrace, and they shall
be cut off in the sight of their people; he has uncovered his
sister's nakedness, he shall be subject to punishment. [18] If
a man lies with a woman having her sickness and uncovers
her nakedness, he has laid bare her flow and she has laid bare
her flow of blood; both of them shall be cut off from their
people. [19] You shall not uncover the nakedness of your mother's sister or of your father's sister, for that is to lay bare one's
own flesh; they shall be subject to punishment. [20] If a man lies
with his uncle's wife, he has uncovered his uncle's nakedness;
they shall be subject to punishment; they shall die childless.
[21] If a man takes his brother's wife, it is impurity; he has
uncovered his brother's nakedness; they shall be childless.

[22] You shall keep all my statutes and all my ordinances, and
observe them, so that the land to which I bring you to settle
in may not vomit you out. [23] You shall not follow the practices
of the nation that I am driving out before you. Because they
did all these things, I abhorred them. [24] But I have said to you:
You shall inherit their land, and I will give it to you to possess,
a land flowing with milk and honey. I am the LORD your God;
I have separated you from the peoples. [25] You shall therefore
make a distinction between the clean animal and the unclean,
and between the unclean bird and the clean; you shall not
bring abomination on yourselves by animal or by bird or by
anything with which the ground teems, which I have set apart
for you to hold unclean. [26] You shall be holy to me; for I the
LORD am holy, and I have separated you from the other
peoples to be mine. [27] A man or a woman who is a medium
or a wizard shall be put to death; they shall be stoned to
death, their blood is upon them.

Much of Leviticus 20 is a mirror image to chapter 18, with the addition of punishments and penalties for the actions prohibited. Many commentators do not provide any information or research on this chapter, simply pointing the reader back to chapter 18.[48] These chapters are very similar, with every prohibition in chapter 20 having a parallel in 18, and in a few occasions chapter 19.[49]

The death penalty is prescribed nine times in this chapter. The offenses assigned this punishment are:

Verse 2: for giving a child to Molech
Verse 9: for cursing your mother or father
Verse 10: for committing adultery

Verse 11: for a man lying with his father's wife
Verse 12: for a man lying with his daughter-in-law
Verse 13: for a man who lies with a male as with a woman
Verse 15: for a man who has sexual relations with an animal
Verse 16: for a woman who has sexual relations with an animal
Verse 27: for a man or a woman who is a medium or a wizard

Verse 9 provides the death penalty for cursing one's parents. This offense is listed just prior to a string of sexually related activities. There is a distinct link between the importance and reverence of family and familial structures, and what the writers of Leviticus took as threats to those families and familial structures—the link being sexual acts that do not lead to procreation.[50] By cursing one's parents or engaging in one of these prohibited sexual acts, the family unit's integrity was being threatened, thereby threatening the society the authors of Leviticus were attempting to protect.[51] These offenses were viewed as demeaning and destructive to the authority and integrity of the patriarchal family structure. Leviticus assigns the death penalty to the deliberate discounting of a parent's authority, as well as sexual conduct that did not have procreation as its main purpose. This punishment is a clear indication of how egregious these kinds of conduct were considered.[52]

These actions were not only a threat to the established social structure, but were directly tied to Israel's possession of the Promised Land. Leviticus 20:22 says, "You shall keep all my statutes and all my ordinances, and observe them, so that the land to which I bring you to settle in may not vomit you out." This verse says that the strict rules and punishments that set the people of Israel apart from those around them had to be followed for the people to keep the land they were about to enter.[53] As seen earlier, the placement of Leviticus between Exodus and Numbers interrupts the flow of the story of the Pentateuch where the Israelite people are about to enter the Promised Land, which indicates the importance of these rules, regulations, and punishments. It also is a way the final assemblers of the Torah could explain how God's chosen people lost the land that was promised to them. It is believed by most commentators that the final form of the Pentateuch took shape while Israel was in exile and had already lost possession of the Promised Land.[54]

So much of the content of Leviticus is striving to make the people of Israel "holy." For Israel to be "holy" it must accept these Levitical codes of behavior that encompass all areas of human conduct: religious practice, civil law, ethical and sexual behavior, and agricultural practices.[55] The reason the death penalty is applied to so many of these offenses is to force the people of Israel to be "holy" in the eyes of God, as interpreted by the author(s) of Leviticus, through the fear of death.[56]

Of the nine offenses to which the death penalty is assigned in chapter 20, six of them have the phrase "their (his) blood is upon them (him)" appended to the description of the offense. These verses are:

Verse 9: for cursing your mother or father
Verse 11: for a man lying with his father's wife
Verse 12: for a man lying with his daughter-in-law
Verse 13: for a man who lies with a male as with a woman
Verse 16: for a woman who has sexual relations with an animal
Verse 27: for a man or a woman who is a medium or a wizard

For these offenses assigned the death penalty, the belief was that the perpetrators had no one else to blame but themselves.[57] The offenses that have the death penalty assigned but do not have the appended phrase "their (his) blood is upon them (him)" are: giving a child to Molech (verse 2), a man committing adultery (verse 10), and a man having sex with an animal (verse 15). At first glance this appears to be an odd assortment of offenses on which not to place sole blame for the punishment. When these three are looked at more closely with the mores of the time in mind, they all involve a patriarchal view of the world taking advantage of someone or something that had no rights. Children had no rights and were considered property. A man who committed adultery with a woman, the woman being someone who was outside the family structure, was a person who had limited to no legal rights and was considered property. A man having sex with an animal (as opposed to a woman) again involves a man using property. Although the importance of procreation in the establishment of these rules is not included in this conclusion, the importance of procreation and the growth of a culturally independent and distinct Israelite society must be balanced with the understanding of a male-dominated society, whose power base needed to be kept inviolable.

Part Three: Discussion

Leviticus is the middle book of the first five books of the people of Israel, known as the Pentateuch or the Torah. It interrupts the narrative story of Israel, just before the people are to enter into the land promised them by God. Much of Leviticus presents directives and instructions as if God were speaking directly to the community about ritual and how social actions and activities can and do impact that ritual.[58] Almost every prohibition in Leviticus 18 and 20 is focused entirely on men and their actions: all these rules and regulations revolve around ritual and purity before God regarding these actions. In Leviticus, human sexuality is considered part of that ritual and part of keeping Israel separate and distinct from the communities that surrounded them. These efforts by the Israelite people would aid them in retaining the land God was about to gift to them.[59]

The rules and laws of Leviticus were written for a people of a certain time and place, and related closely to a very particular society, in a very particular set of circumstances: having just completed forty years of wandering in the desert and being about to enter their Promised Land.[60] Remember that these rules were written for a people in exile who had already lost that land and their leaders were seeking understanding for that loss. That is not to say that these rules and regulations should not be taken seriously. Yet they must be looked at as a whole piece of cloth first, not simply as individual threads to be studied irrespective of the fabric around them.

Certainly modern society will find some of the rules and laws in Leviticus strange, unusual, and in fact a denigration of humanity, and in particular female physicality.[61] The book comes from an era where much of sexual activity was exploitive, violent, and in many cases connected with cultic practices. As discussed in chapter 1 of this book, sex was very much about power, domination, and strength.

The language utilized in Leviticus 18:22 and 20:13, "shall not lie with a male as with a woman," is indicative of this understanding and attitude toward sexual acts. For a man to act as a woman, to allow himself to be dominated, "taken" so to speak, went against the societal structures and understandings of role and place in society. To place oneself in that position was to step outside of a rigidly maintained hierarchy. Such action blurred what was considered appropriate dealings between society's hierarchal strata.[62] When sex has to do with power and position in society, laws and rules were needed to keep that societal structure in place. Thus, much of Leviticus has to do with keeping those societal structures clear and understandable to the society for whom it was written. Add to this the priestly class need to make the people of Israel "holy," multitudinous, and separate and distinct from the societies that surrounded Israel. When placed in that context, the rules about sexual activity take on a different understanding.

It is important to note that these prohibitions make no mention of women lying with women. Women were considered at this time in this culture to be of a lower status, the property of either their fathers or their husbands. They were not individuals upon whom the society relied for keeping the social order. Any sexual conduct between women did not compromise the patriarchal societal structure. No prohibition against women lying with women would have been deemed necessary.

It was not solely sexual acts that were considered an abomination to the society reflected in Leviticus. The eating of certain types of food, the sowing of different kinds of seeds in the same field, the wearing of different types of cloth at the same time, were all considered detestable[63] in order to keep things in a neat, orderly, and understandable manner, thereby being able to explain and comprehend the world surrounding that culture and society. The priestly cult that created Leviticus wanted the Israelite people to be separate and distinct, and notably apart from, the society which surrounded them. These rules facilitated that desire.

"Lying with" and "abomination" regarding male on male conduct were considered something different from "seeing the nakedness of," or sexual activity, by the authors of Leviticus. The prohibitions in Leviticus 18:22 and 20:13 were not about sex and sexual relations as we understand them in the twenty-first century. These prohibitions had to do with keeping a rigid and male-dominated society distinct from that which surrounded it: to clearly delineate roles and societal rules.

Leviticus 18:22 and 20:13 were written for a certain time and a particular culture and context. They are just one piece of the puzzle of the Pentateuch, and the society that existed at that place and time. Taken in context, these passages can be seen as an attempt to make sense of a society, to protect a society and culture that was trying to be built, and protect a class and style of life distinct from others around them. This patriarchal society, and the social structures emanating from them, would experience their worldview as threatened by conduct that did not fit into this rigid and male-dominated society.

Much of sex and sexual relations as we understand them in the twenty-first century are different from what was experienced and understood when Leviticus was written. Sexual conduct was predominately about taking, power, and what we would consider today rape. To utilize these verses in Leviticus as weapons of condemnation against people who have been made in God's image is a disservice to the text, a misuse of the Torah, and an insult to God's Word as it is made known to us. God's Word is not meant to be frozen in time. It is to be heard anew today and looked at with fresh perspective and understanding based on the world that is hearing these words anew, remembering God created out of love, not restriction or dislike.

CHAPTER THREE

Romans 1

Paul, a servant of Jesus Christ, called to be an apostle, set
apart for the gospel of God, [2] which he promised beforehand
through his prophets in the holy scriptures, [3] the gospel concerning his Son, who was descended from David according
to the flesh [4] and was declared to be Son of God with power
according to the spirit of holiness by resurrection from the
dead, Jesus Christ our Lord, [5] through whom we have received
grace and apostleship to bring about the obedience of faith
among all the Gentiles for the sake of his name, [6] including
yourselves who are called to belong to Jesus Christ, [7] To all
God's beloved in Rome, who are called to be saints: Grace to
you and peace from God our Father and the Lord Jesus Christ.
[8] First, I thank my God through Jesus Christ for all of you,
because your faith is proclaimed throughout the world. [9] For
God, whom I serve with my spirit by announcing the gospel
of his Son, is my witness that without ceasing I remember
you always in my prayers, [10] asking that by God's will I may
somehow at last succeed in coming to you. [11] For I am longing
to see you so that I may share with you some spiritual gift to
strengthen you— [12] or rather so that we may be mutually

encouraged by each other's faith, both yours and mine.
13 I want you to know, brothers and sisters, that I have often
intended to come to you (but thus far have been prevented),
in order that I may reap some harvest among you as I have
among the rest of the Gentiles. 14 I am a debtor both to
Greeks and to barbarians, both to the wise and to the foolish
15 —hence my eagerness to proclaim the gospel to you also
who are in Rome. 16 For I am not ashamed of the gospel; it is
the power of God for salvation to everyone who has faith, to
the Jew first and also to the Greek. 17 For in it the righteousness of God is revealed through faith for faith; as it is written,
"The one who is righteous will live by faith." 18 For the wrath
of God is revealed from heaven against all ungodliness and
wickedness of those who by their wickedness suppress the
truth. 19 For what can be known about God is plain to them,
because God has shown it to them. 20 Ever since the creation
of the world his eternal power and divine nature, invisible
though they are, have been understood and seen through the
things he has made. So they are without excuse; 21 for though
they knew God, they did not honor him as God or give thanks
to him, but they became futile in their thinking, and their
senseless minds were darkened. 22 Claiming to be wise, they
became fools; 23 and they exchanged the glory of the immortal
God for images resembling a mortal human being or birds or
four-footed animals or reptiles. 24 Therefore God gave them up
in the lusts of their hearts to impurity, to the degrading of their
bodies among themselves, 25 because they exchanged the truth
about God for a lie and worshiped and served the creature
rather than the Creator, who is blessed forever! Amen. 26 For
this reason God gave them up to degrading passions. Their

women exchanged natural intercourse for unnatural, 27 and in
the same way also the men, giving up natural intercourse with
women, were consumed with passion for one another. Men
committed shameless acts with men and received in their
own persons the due penalty for their error. 28 And since they
did not see fit to acknowledge God, God gave them up to a
debased mind and to things that should not be done. 29 They
were filled with every kind of wickedness, evil, covetousness,
malice. Full of envy, murder, strife, deceit, craftiness, they are
gossips, 30 slanderers, God-haters, insolent, haughty, boastful,
inventors of evil, rebellious toward parents, 31 foolish, faithless,
heartless, ruthless. 32 They know God's decree, that those who
practice such things deserve to die—yet they not only do them
but even applaud others who practice them.

Paul's letter to the Romans, and in fact all of Paul's writings, poses interesting and different issues than we saw in the Hebrew Testament texts. I am using the same textual interpretation approaches: reading the verses of interest in context to the entirety of the writing; understanding the context and culture in which it was written; and looking at how the principles set forth can be understood in today's world. We know more about Paul and the world he inhabited than we do the eras that Genesis, Judges, and Leviticus represent. This knowledge allows us to address questions more fully, chief among those, at least for this letter, is that we know the identity of the author.

How do we understand these words in 1:26–27 that can seem so harsh to some? At the beginning of Paul's longest letter these verses carry a tremendous influence. Former archbishop of Canterbury, Lord Carey, cited them as "scripturally dispositive on the issue of homosexuality as an illegitimate and condemned lifestyle."[1] A holistic understanding of the letter to the Romans bolsters the ability to reflect on their meaning.

Although this letter is placed as the first of Paul's letters as they are set out in the Bible, it is nearly the unanimous consent of commentators that Romans was Paul's last letter and, unusual for Paul, written to a community he had neither founded nor visited.[2] Romans 1:26–27 have no textual variants, the presence of which would further cloud our understanding.[3]

The basic structure of this letter follows Paul's usual format. Chapter 1 sets forth an opening greeting, a thanksgiving, and the statement of his overarching theme—the righteousness of God—followed by the body of the letter, which contains numerous subthemes.[4] The first section of the letter involves doctrinal matters: God's wrath at Jewish and Gentile sinfulness (1:18–3:20); Paul's discussion of the justification by faith apart from the law (3:21–4:25); God's salvation of those who have faith (5:1–8:39); and God's promises to Israel (9:1–11:36). In the next section, Paul provides advice for appropriate Christian living (12:1–13:14); and speaks to the importance of the strong having compassion for the weak (14:1–15:13). Paul ends the letter by enumerating his hoped-for travel plans, provides blessings and greetings to specific people, and concludes with a doxology (15:14–16:27).[5]

Romans 1:26–27 is part of the first section of the body of the letter: God's anger at Jewish and Gentile sinfulness. There is a certain surprise to this opening part of the letter. To understand this startling opening, we need to explore the earlier verses as well as what comes right after chapter 1.[6]

Even though the general format of Romans is like Paul's other letters, there is disagreement about if this letter is a general theological letter, or whether it is situational and directed to a community with a focus or pastoral problem in mind.[7]

However we look at this letter, Paul is doing something different than we see in his other letters.[8] He is utilizing a creative writing style that can cause his message to be misconstrued if that writing technique is not recognized: a masterful rhetorical style aimed at persuading his readers to think in a certain way. Rhetoric is defined by the *Merriam-Webster Online Dictionary* as

> the art of speaking or writing effectively: such as (a): the study of principles and rules of composition formulated by critics of ancient times (b): the study of writing or speaking as a means of communication or persuasion.

This letter, and in particular the first and second chapters of it, is a prime example of the art of rhetorical writing as an "instrument of persuasion."[9] It exemplifies how Paul had a mastery of rhetorical theory and how well versed he was in the ability to utilize rhetoric to enhance and emphasize a particular point for a specific audience.[10] Whether or not this letter is considered a general theological exposition or one that is directed at a particular audience, Paul is making a strong and focused argument about a God-centered community life.

It is important to note that when Paul wrote this letter, he did not designate individual chapters; it was one long letter. The chapter divisions were added in later years. To look at a portion of chapter 1, ignoring what comes right after it, misses the thrust of Paul's argument and gives artificial weight to chapter headings. Paul states the overarching thesis of the letter in 1:16–17:

> For I am not ashamed of the gospel; it is the power of God for salvation to everyone who has faith, to the Jew first and also to the Greek. [17] For in it the righteousness of God is revealed through faith for faith; as it is written, "The one who is righteous will live by faith."

This thesis statement leads into the first part of the body of the letter where Paul addresses doctrinal matters. In this section Paul talks about the "wrath of God" (Romans 1:18). This wrath of God leads to the strong condemnation Paul seemingly levels at the Gentile world but turns out to be a trap for the unwary reader. Whether that reader be Gentile or Jewish, this trap can be activated based on what immediately follows in Romans 2: a condemnation of the self-righteous.[11] To understand this rhetorical trap, a detailed review of verses 18–32 is necessary.

> 18 For the wrath of God is revealed from heaven against all
> ungodliness and wickedness of those who by their wick-
> edness suppress the truth. 19 For what can be known about
> God is plain to them, because God has shown it to them.
> 20 Ever since the creation of the world his eternal power and
> divine nature, invisible though they are, have been under-
> stood and seen through the things he has made. So they are
> without excuse; 21 for though they knew God, they did not
> honor him as God or give thanks to him, but they became
> futile in their thinking, and their senseless minds were
> darkened. 22 Claiming to be wise, they became fools; 23 and
> they exchanged the glory of the immortal God for images
> resembling a mortal human being or birds or four-footed
> animals or reptiles.

God's plan is clear to all of God's creation, according to verses 19–20, and God's creation has no excuse not to understand or obey God's plan. Paul's condemnation of Roman society and culture starts in verse 21, "for though they knew God, they did not honor him" becoming "futile in their thinking." The key to the following verses of this chapter resides in verses 21 and 23: although "they knew God," "they exchanged the glory of the immortal God for images resembling a mortal human being or birds or four-footed animals or reptiles."[12] Here is the key to understanding the remainder of this chapter. Paul is using idolatrous language, which signals his intent. Idol worship led God to "deliver" or "gave them up" to the vices listed in the following verses.[13] Paul uses the same Greek word (*paradidomi*) to refer to the idol worship vilified, but translators present in three different ways: to "deliver," "gave them up," or "gave them over." In biblical writing, whenever an author repeats a word in a closely defined part of the text, the reader's ears should perk up. The author is sending a signal. This signal is easily missed because the translators used different translations for the same Greek word (perhaps for stylistic reasons). In this grouping of verses, Paul is saying that God is doing the work; it is God who delivered them up. *Paradidomi* means "delivered" or "gave them up" or "gave them over." God gave these people up; God delivered these people over to these actions because of their idol worship. Their actions are not Paul's focal point. He is leading the reader to focus on the improper worship of God. Following his accusation of idol worship, he says:

> 24 *Therefore* God *gave them up* in the lusts of their hearts
> to impurity, to the degrading of their bodies among them-
> selves, 25 because they exchanged the truth about God for
> a lie and worshiped and served the creature rather than the
> Creator, who is blessed forever! Amen. (emphasis added)

The use of "therefore" (*dio*) serves as a link to God's action and reaction to the prior conduct of humankind and links the first of the three of God's "giving up" (*paradidomi*) to that conduct (idol worship), which is more explicitly stated in verse 25. The second use of *paradidomi* comes in verse 26:

> 26 *For this reason* God *gave them up* to degrading passions.
> Their women exchanged natural intercourse for unnatural,
> 27 and in the same way also the men, *giving up* natural
> intercourse with women, were consumed with passion for
> one another. Men committed shameless acts with men and
> received in their own persons the due penalty for their error.
> (emphasis added)

The prepositional phrase at the beginning of verse 26 "for this reason" (*dia*) directly links God's "giving (them) up," as well as the conduct in verse 27, to the prior idol worshipping conduct being condemned. The third use of *paradidomi* appears in verses 28–32:

> [28] *And* since they did not see fit to acknowledge God, God
> *gave them up* to a debased mind and to things that should
> not be done. [29] They were filled with every kind of wicked-
> ness, evil, covetousness, malice. Full of envy, murder, strife,
> deceit, craftiness, they are gossips, [30] slanderers, God-hat-
> ers,[f] insolent, haughty, boastful, inventors of evil, rebel-
> lious toward parents, [31] foolish, faithless, heartless, ruth-
> less. [32] They know God's decree, that those who practice
> such things deserve to die—yet they not only do them but
> even applaud others who practice them. (emphasis added)

The first of the "giving up" by God was on the religious and mental level of worshiping a creature rather then the creator. The second is God giving them up on a sexual level. The third delivers them up on a "public level in the form of criminal and sociopathic behavior."[14] These actions by God's creation are God's doing in delivering up God's creation to passions which would be understood to be reviled by Jewish and Christian communities of that time. The fundamental failure of human beings is the rejection of God and the failure to worship God. This is the root of all the failings enumerated above—failings that God has allowed to continue as the people did not worship and honor God appropriately.[15]

Paul's use of the word *paradidomi* is a powerful choice of words in describing God's action regarding the idol worshipping conduct of the individuals who should have known better. The word is utilized in all four Gospels to describe Jesus's being handed over, delivered up, given up to crucifixion.

Matthew 27:26: So he released Barabbas for them; and after flogging Jesus, he handed him over to be crucified.

Mark 15:15: So Pilate, wishing to satisfy the crowd, released Barabbas for them; and after flogging Jesus, he handed him over to be crucified.

Luke 23:25: He released the man they asked for, the one who had been put in prison for insurrection and murder, and he handed Jesus over as they wished.

John 19:16: Then he handed him over to them to be crucified. So they took Jesus;

John 19:30: When Jesus had received the wine, he said, "It is finished." Then he bowed his head and gave up his spirit.

This form of the word is utilized eight times in the Gospels, and ninety-seven times in the Hebrew Testament. In nearly all the cases in the Hebrew Testament, the work being accomplished, the one doing the handing over, is done by God: there is a divine intervention in these actions.[16] The same can be said for the word's usage in the Gospels. Although Paul's letter to the Romans was written before the four Gospels, the use of this word *paradidomi* gives the action significance; the actions to which the individuals are being handed over are God's doing, not their own. In the Matthew, Mark, Luke, and John, Pilate is handing Jesus over for crucifixion. This "handing over" is God's ultimate sacrifice of the God-self and God's son. Jesus's handing over of his spirit in John 19:30 is the conclusion of that sacrifice. The utilization of this word *paradidomi* in Romans carries tremendous significance.

In all of God's "giving up" in Romans 1, Paul does not mention sin. Sin is not mentioned by Paul until Romans 3:9. Similarly, after the initial salutation and thanksgiving, Jesus is not mentioned in chapters 1 or 2 and does not make an appearance until the end of chapter 3.[17] This unusual pattern for Paul is one that should make the reader aware that he is up to something different than in his other letters. By leaving Jesus out of this initial part of the letter, Paul may be assisting the reader in falling into the rhetorical trap he is setting, which he snaps shut at the beginning of chapter 2.

All the things to which Paul points in 1:24–32 are God's doing because of the people's choice of worshipping idols: God allowed these religious, sexual, and societal failures to continue. The people made a choice to worship idols and God "gave them up" to those states of being. This is an interesting tension. It resonates with the tension that exists in much of Paul's writing: the tension between Paul's belief that God is the God of Israel, and that God provides salvation only in Jesus.[18] Much of Paul's writing shows how he lived trying to explain and understand the tension, although Paul did not need to explain, or think out, his own faith. After all, Paul did not think his way into the Christian faith; he came to his faith in a revelatory manner on the road to Damascus and spent the better part of his life wrestling with this tension.[19] Verses 26 and 27 say in part (emphasis added):

> 26: Their women exchanged natural *intercourse* for *unnatural*,
> 27: and in the same way also the men, giving up natural *intercourse* with women, were consumed with passion for one another.

The Greek word chosen by Paul, translated as intercourse, is *chresis,* which means "to use, to function as," and is found in the New Testament only in a sexual sense. It is also translated as "utilization."[20] The words "use," "function as," and "utilization" have a demeaning connotation when they are used in a sexual sense. Utilizing or using someone for sexual release does not imply mutuality, or commonality of desire. With this understanding in mind, this word gives a more difficult reading of the action Paul is criticizing. This word *chresis* is utilized seven times in the Bible. In all cases, the word has the meaning of "use," as in some object being used for a purpose.[21] There is nothing in the selection of this word that steers toward an understanding of mutuality in the sexual activity being described. There is nothing loving or mutual.[22]

In verse 26 the Greek words translated "unnatural" are *para phusis*, which literally means "contrary to nature" or "besides/alongside nature."[23] Another way to translate this phrase is "besides what is expected."[24] Paul utilizes this exact phrase in Romans 11:24 when he describes the grafting of the Gentiles onto the Jewish olive tree (emphasis added):

> For if you have been cut from what is *by nature* a wild olive tree and grafted, *contrary to nature*, into a cultivated olive tree, how much more will these natural branches be grafted back into their own olive tree.

Paul describes a grafting where Gentiles, who are not Jewish, get inserted into Israel and its promises through Jesus. By use of the same phrase to describe queer sexual activity and the union of Gentiles and Jews onto one olive tree, Paul is not saying they are the same things. The usage of those words serves Paul's rhetorical purpose of setting the snare of the trap for the unwary reader. The use of *para phusis* helps put in context Paul's usage of queer sexual activity in setting up the conversation to follow.[25]

Although Paul appears to be condemning the behavior of Gentile Christians in his condemnations in 1:23–32, he is also arguing to the Jewish community utilizing language, traditions, symbols, and behaviors they will readily understand.[26] The vices that Paul accuses people of having adopted, to which they have been given up to by God, are the consequence of their rejection of God, and their failure to worship God appropriately. All are rooted in idolatry and the rejection of God. Paul is relying on the Wisdom of Solomon (14:27) where all sins come from idolatry: "for the worship of idols not to be named is the source and cause and end of every evil."[27] Here is another piece of the trap that Paul is setting for the unwary reader: his reliance on concepts that would be familiar to the intended audience, conduct they could understand as against their society's norms.[28]

Paul is not trying to prove that the conduct cited was perverse or wrong; he assumed that as a given to his audience. The conduct Paul condemns is the result of God's anger, not the reason for it.[29] In Paul's mind, the only reason for sexual relations is a divinely constructed plan for males and females to reproduce. To Paul, sex has no other purpose. Pleasure was not part of Paul's vocabulary when it came to discussing sex.[30] To his cultural mindset, the vices he lists are the manifestations of God's wrath for idolatrous behavior.[31] Queer sexual activity, at least to Paul, was contrary to God's creative purpose of procreation, and no other, and this point would have been evident to his initial readers.[32] It is important to recognize that the listing of all these vices is not his primary focus; the passage focuses, in a fundamental way, on the relationship between God and human beings. There is no subsequent mention of queer sexual relations in this letter, indicating that this is not his point.[33] Paul is simply highlighting a given, based on his worldview of the society in which he lived and to which he wrote. The focus of this portion of Romans is the appropriate honoring of God.

By dishonoring God, Paul picks up on a theme from some of his other letters. In particular he focuses on the idea of the importance of life in the body. In 1 Corinthians 6:13 and 15:35–39, Paul describes how important bodily existence is because we are destined to share the risen life of Jesus. By dishonoring the body, the individual is doing grievous injury to this later union with Jesus and to one's present union with him.[34] And yet, Paul does not say that men or women who engage in "unnatural" passion injure God; because of their idol worship these actions and urges are given to them by God and are self-injurious. There is no punishment set by God. The punishment, as Paul sees it, is the act itself. Verse 27 is translated in the NRSV as:

> and in the same way also the men, giving up natural intercourse with women, were consumed with passion for one another. Men committed shameless acts with men and received in their own persons the due penalty for their error.

Another translation of this same verse sheds a different understanding:

> and likewise also the males, after they abandoned the natural use with females, were inflamed with their lust for one another, males who work up their shameful member in (other) males, and receive back for their deception the recompense that is tightness in themselves.[35]

In Paul's time and culture, male bodies were thought of as hard, stiff, and nonabsorbent. Female bodies were considered loose, soft, and absorbent. Female bodies, based on this understanding, could absorb ejaculate where the male body would only become sore. The punishment for male sexual acts with other males was not only the act itself but also the resulting soreness caused by the act.[36] The bottom line to Paul is that this kind of sexual activity does not create children and is therefore out of bounds. Idolatry does not lead just to a spiritual barrenness but also has a physical aspect, a physical pain to it, a physical barrenness as well.[37]

The dishonoring of the body and the disordering of society to which human beings are given up by God exist as equally grave punishments for improperly worshiping God. The sexual practices condemned by Paul are on a par with the destructiveness of "wickedness, evil, covetousness, malice, . . . envy, murder, strife, deceit, craftiness, they are gossips, slanderers, God-haters, insolent, haughty, boastful, inventors of evil, rebellious toward parents, foolish, faithless, heartless, ruthless" (1:29–30).[38] The equalizing of these actions is a deliberate rhetorical shaping of the text by Paul to enable him to "spring his trap." Just when the reader thinks there is safety in feeling content that Paul is not addressing them, for they certainly do not do these things, Paul springs his rhetorical trap meant to catch those who condemn people and yet, in some way, "do the very same things" (chapter 2:1, 3).[39] In doing so, Paul utilizes language from Psalm 106:20 and Jeremiah 2:11.

Ps. 106:20: They exchanged the glory of God for the image of an ox that eats grass.

Jer. 2:11 Has a nation changed its gods, even though they are no gods? But my people have changed their glory for something that does not profit.

Both of these verses address Israelite piety and idolatry. By utilizing this language Paul is, once again, making use of things that would be familiar to many of his original listeners. It would have appeared to many a reader of the letter that they were safe and secure and not in Paul's line of fire. But the beginning of chapter 2 changes that:

> Therefore you have no excuse, whoever you are, when you judge others; *for in passing judgment on another you condemn yourself*, because *you*, the judge, *are doing the very same things*. (emphasis added)[40]

Paul accuses Jew and Gentile alike of not worshiping God appropriately. The list in chapter 1 of God's "giving over" should not be considered as comprehensive and all-inclusive, but merely illustrative of the kind of behavior that God gives people over to when they do not worship God appropriately: thereby perfecting his trap for the unwary and comfortable reader.[41]

As mentioned previously, there is a split among commentators if Romans was written with a specific reader or community in mind. Some argue that the implied readers are Jewish Christians, while others claim its focus is on Gentile Christians. Others believe, correctly, that Paul is talking to both groups.[42]

The complexity of the letter, its intricate structure and breadth of content, indicate that Paul was trying to reach as wide an audience as possible. This first chapter is a set-up into which both the Gentile and Jewish Christian communities could easily have fallen. Paul's close focus on queer sexual relations would ring very clearly to this audience, thereby allowing his real point to be made at the beginning of chapter 2.[43]

In the society and culture to which Paul was writing, there was a very strong link between idolatry and sexual conduct thought to be pleasing to the "gods" that were being worshiped by those acts. The Gentile and Jewish Christian communities would have been aware of this kind of conduct, and would understand it to be depraved. Paul was also tapping into the concept of a paternalistic society where gender and roles were tightly interwoven: with females being dominated by males. Queer relations would blur the lines of these gender role distinctions central to that society's culture, and would be easily recognized by the readers of Paul's letter as not fitting for the community they were trying to build and maintain.[44] These references to queer sexual relations are not there for their own sake, but serve a rhetorical function: to entrap those who condemn the behavior, but in similar ways, "do the same thing."[45]

In that Greco-Roman world in which the community to which Paul was writing existed, queer sexual relations were a given. It was a part of the cultural life, the religious life, and the political life.[46] In that surrounding culture, "natural intercourse meant the penetration of a subordinate person by a dominant one."[47] Paul is aiming to affirm the values of sex for purposes of "procreation only" by pointing to the conduct of a community surrounding them which followed a different norm.[48] The laws at that time in Rome allowed a master to demand sexual services from any slave, male or female. Sexual relations between masters and their male slaves was a common occurrence, and in accordance with the standards of a male-dominated society.[49] Paul does not seem to take this into account, nor make a distinction between active and passive partners as the Roman culture did. Roman culture was very hierarchal, with those in power having free reign to act out sexually, in any way they wanted, among those who were of a lower cultural and societal standing. Paul is setting forth a countercultural stance for Gentile Christians, many of whom may have been former slaves, or still were slaves and had suffered ill treatment by their masters. Paul may have been offering a soothing balm of hope to those who were forced into those types of encounters.[50]

The knowledge of God's love for us is not something that requires special knowledge, nor is it for a select few. God's love is for all of God's creation. In Romans, Paul makes that point clear: that this knowledge is open to all and given to all of God's creation. Paul says in verses 19 and 20, "for what can be known about God is plain to them because God has shown them" and "they are without excuse" for not worshiping God.[51] Further along in Romans, Paul makes this point even more explicit. In Romans 10:8–13 Paul says:

> But what does it say? "The word is near you, on your lips and in your heart" (that is, the word of faith that we proclaim); 9 because if you confess with your lips that Jesus is Lord and believe in your heart that God raised him from the dead, you will be saved. 10 For one believes with the heart and so is justified, and one confesses with the mouth and so is saved. 11 The scripture says, "*No one* who believes in him will be put to shame." 12 For there is no distinction between Jew and Greek; the same Lord is Lord of *all* and is generous to *all* who call on him. 13 For, "*Everyone* who calls on the name of the Lord shall be saved." (emphasis added)

Knowing what we do about the society and culture to whom Paul was writing, we can see his desire to keep the Christian community, both Gentile and Jewish, separate and distinct from those that surrounded them. With the broader knowledge of his masterful use of rhetoric in this first chapter of Romans, it is inappropriate and a misuse of the text to jury-pick Paul's reference to queer sexual relations and utilize it as a condemnation of all queer people. Paul was utilizing a literary device to point people in the direction of the proper worship of God. Paul was arguing from the point of view that sex was for procreation and nothing else, and the focus of the chapter is the proper worship of God.

Paul says that God gave these idol worshipers over to acting in a manner that would have been inappropriate to the community to whom he was writing. Acting not only sexually but with "wickedness . . . envy, murder, strife . . . craftiness . . . gossips . . . slanderers . . . haughty . . . rebellious to parents . . . foolish . . . ruthless" (verses 29–31). Certainly, at the beginning of chapter 2 Paul is not accusing the people he is writing to of orgies; he is accusing them of the inappropriate worship of God. The vices listed are the result of their being "handed over" by God to those actions.

The kind of sexual activity that existed at the time Paul was writing was from a patriarchal, male-dominated viewpoint in a society severely stratified by class, role, and status. Those in the lower strata of society were treated unequally and abusively: physically, psychologically, and sexually.[52] This cultural overlay is an important lens to understanding this text. The prevailing mindset tolerated the taking of another individual in what we would consider today as rape and a violent misuse and abuse of others. Surely there were love and emotions between people, but the structure of society was based on power, with violent conduct being just one way to use and abuse it. The society was structured in such a stratified way that power rested with the "strong," with the "higher" classes who had the right to take whatever they wanted. Although there are areas of the world where power and sex are intertwined in this old and abhorrent way, they are not thought of as modern and are in fact blighted.

Paul's rhetorical literary device should not be utilized to condemn queer sexual relations. Doing so allows us to fall into Paul's trap of judging others. Paul's selection of the word *chresis* ("to use," "utilization") proves that Paul is making a rhetorical stab at the heart of the Roman community: they must worship God appropriately and not "use" each other. Paul is not talking about mutuality or love in Romans 1. He is talking about use, and misuse, of power and authority, and how that impacts one's relationship with God. He is talking about violence and a wrongful taking, and how those impact one's relationship with God. Paul is pointing his readers to a proper relationship with God, demanding they put away false idols that can and do corrupt that relationship with God.

CHAPTER FOUR

1 Corinthians 6

When any of you has a grievance against another, do you dare
to take it to court before the unrighteous, instead of taking it
before the saints? [2] Do you not know that the saints will judge
the world? And if the world is to be judged by you, are you
incompetent to try trivial cases? [3] Do you not know that we
are to judge angels—to say nothing of ordinary matters? [4] If
you have ordinary cases, then, do you appoint as judges those
who have no standing in the church? [5] I say this to your shame.
Can it be that there is no one among you wise enough to
decide between one believer and another, [6] but a believer goes
to court against a believer—and before unbelievers at that?
[7] In fact, to have lawsuits at all with one another is already a
defeat for you. Why not rather be wronged? Why not rather
be defrauded? [8] But you yourselves wrong and defraud—and
believers at that. [9] Do you not know that wrongdoers will not
inherit the kingdom of God? Do not be deceived! Fornicators,
idolaters, adulterers, male prostitutes, sodomites, [10] thieves,
the greedy, drunkards, revilers, robbers—none of these will
inherit the kingdom of God. [11] And this is what some of you
used to be. But you were washed, you were sanctified, you

were justified in the name of the Lord Jesus Christ and in the
Spirit of our God. [12] "All things are lawful for me," but not
all things are beneficial. "All things are lawful for me," but
I will not be dominated by anything. [13] "Food is meant for the
stomach and the stomach for food," and God will destroy both
one and the other. The body is meant not for fornication but
for the Lord, and the Lord for the body. [14] And God raised the
Lord and will also raise us by his power. [15] Do you not know
that your bodies are members of Christ? Should I therefore
take the members of Christ and make them members of a
prostitute? Never! [16] Do you not know that whoever is united
to a prostitute becomes one body with her? For it is said,
"The two shall be one flesh." [17] But anyone united to the
Lord becomes one spirit with him. [18] Shun fornication! Every
sin that a person commits is outside the body; but the fornicator sins against the body itself. [19] Or do you not know that
your body is a temple of the Holy Spirit within you, which
you have from God, and that you are not your own? [20] For you
were bought with a price; therefore glorify God in your body.

Following his visit to Antioch in Syria, Corinth was the first major city where Paul established a church mission. He lived in Corinth for eighteen months establishing house churches. Paul's visit and vision helped create the community, allowing it to flourish and grow.[1] In writing the Corinthians this first of two letters, Paul was responding to at least one letter he had received in which the people in this community asked Paul questions about suitable conduct in general, and the appropriateness of certain conduct by individuals in the community.

A rough outline of the entire letter, which is Paul's response to those inquiries, would be: the opening and thanksgiving (1:1–9), issues regarding devotion (1:10–4:21), what to do with a man living with his stepmother (chapter 5), legal disputes (6:1–11), sexual relations and marriage (6:12–7:40), on eating food that has been sacrificed to idols (8:1–11:1), procedures for the Lord's Supper (11:17–34), spiritual gifts (chapters 12–14), the resurrection of the dead (chapter 15), and giving money to Jerusalem (chapter 16).[2] This letter addresses a wide-range of issues.

1 Corinthians 6:1–11 sits right in between an exhortation on the how to deal with a man living with his stepmother, and another on marriage and sexual relations/obligations of the parties who are married. First Conrinthians 6:1–11 can be divided into two units: lawsuits between Christians (vv. 1–8), and behaviors and vices that concern Paul (vv. 9–11). This list of behaviors in 6:9–11 is expanded from a similar list in the preceding chapter.[3] Some argue that 1 Corinthians 5, 6, and 7 are one pericope divided into sections. Others say they are separate but interrelated units, with each unit able to stand on its own. Chapter 5 focuses on what Paul considered an intolerable situation: a man living in a scandalous manner with his stepmother. Paul focuses on judgment and punishment because of that kind of conduct.[4] The beginning of chapter 6 addresses the appropriateness of legal suits. These verses are related to the forgoing as they focus on judging and judgment, but from a different perspective.[5]

The instructions on not being involved with the legal system in the surrounding community closely tie in with Paul's primary focus on sexual morality. He is concentrating on the failure of the Corinthians to act as a community, to act as a cohesive whole that is interested in each other's well-being, and not being self-centered individuals like those of the surrounding community.[6] Being set apart from the surrounding community's culture is a common theme in Paul's letters. Chapter 6 is a linchpin in Paul's directions concerning sexual morality. It is a concrete example of how Paul expects a community should operate in judging itself and its constituent members.[7] The repetition of behaviors set forth in chapter 6, with some additional ones added in, is a clear example of the interdependence of the chapters and how Paul is building an argument, step by step.[8]

The first eleven verses of chapter 6 repeat the phrase "Do you not know" three times. "Do you not know that the saints will judge the world?" (6:2). "Do you not know that we are to judge angels—to say nothing of ordinary matters?" (6:3). Do you not know that wrongdoers will not inherit the kingdom of God?" (6:9). Paul's tone is lively and indignant, asking ten questions about lawsuits and focusing on what he considered to be wrongdoing.[9] Faithful attention to these twelve verses will show that it is inappropriate to use this text to condemn one or two of the "sinners" listed in Paul's vice list, when the focus of the passage is on litigation and greed and not sex.[10]

Verses 9 and 10 provide some interesting translation issues.

NRSV: 9 Do you not know that wrongdoers will not inherit the kingdom of God? Do not be deceived! Fornicators, idolaters, adulterers, *male prostitutes, sodomites*, 10 thieves, the greedy, drunkards, revilers, robbers—none of these will inherit the kingdom of God.

NASB: 9 Or do you not know that the unrighteous will not inherit the kingdom of God? Do not be deceived; neither the sexually immoral, nor idolaters, nor adulterers, *nor homosexuals*, 10 nor thieves, nor the greedy, nor those habitually drunk, nor verbal abusers, nor swindlers, will inherit the kingdom of God.

ESV: 9 Do you not know that the unrighteous will not inherit the kingdom of God? Do not be deceived: neither the sexually immoral, nor idolaters, nor adulterers, *nor men who practice homosexuality*, 10 nor thieves, nor the greedy, nor drunkards, nor revilers, nor swindlers will inherit the kingdom of God.

KJV: 9 Know ye not that the unrighteous shall not inherit the kingdom of God? Be not deceived: neither fornicators, nor idolaters, nor adulterers, *nor effeminate, nor abusers of themselves with mankind*, 10 Nor thieves, nor covetous, nor drunkards, nor revilers, nor extortioners, shall inherit the kingdom of God.

NIV: 9 Do you not know that the wicked will not inherit the kingdom of God? Do not be deceived: Neither the sexually immoral nor idolaters nor adulterers *nor male prostitutes nor homosexual offenders* 10 nor thieves nor the greedy nor drunkards nor slanderers nor swindlers will inherit the kingdom of God.

Here we have five very different translations of the same Greek words: *oute malakos oute arsenokoites*. The word *malakos* literally means "soft ones," "effeminate."[11] This word was sometimes used to refer to male prostitutes, in particular young boys who were the passive partners in pederast relationships with men. This is not the usual word utilized in referring to these young male prostitutes, and this term, *malakos* had a broader and more common pejorative definition that in today's parlance would mean "sissies" or "dandies."[12] Some translate *malakos* as "perverts." Pejoratively this word was used in Hellenistic Greek society to describe the passive partners in a sexual relationship.[13] This pejorative meaning would have been an attack on men who would not act in a culturally "manly" manner.[14] This is likely Paul's intent. The use of the pejorative also fits in with the overall tone of this part of the letter. It is almost as if Paul is raising his voice, first asking "Do you not know" three times and then saying, "You don't really think people like *this* (sissies) will inherit the kingdom of God, do you?"

The second word that has caused some disagreement in translation is *arsenokoites*. It is an unusual word that appears nowhere else in the Bible or, for that matter, in Greek literature. This appears to be a rendering into Greek of a standard rabbinic phrase that literally means "one who lies with a male {as with a woman},"[15] or more specifically "sleeper with males."[16] Paul apparently took the words utilized in Leviticus 18:22 and 20:13 (see chapter 2) and created a word that would be descriptive and understandable to his readers.[17] This word *arsenokoites* would have been used to describe men who were the more "active" member of a same gender sexual relationship. There was common practice, in the time that Paul was writing, for married heterosexual men to keep a boy for sexual pleasure. Some of these individuals were slaves, or from lower classes. None was given a choice about participating in the sexual activity; it was a societal expectation. There were also prostitutes who solicited sex for money, both male and female. In the society that surrounded the community to which Paul was writing, this kind of arrangement and behavior would not have caused any or unusual attention from the culture at large.[18] Prostitution was not only legal, it was a widely accepted social phenomenon. Sexual activity of this kind, whether with boys or women, was not outside the social conventions of the society surrounding these new Christian communities that Paul had founded.[19]

This kind of behavior would have been thought of as anathema to the Jewish community as well as to this new Christian community based in Jewish cultural norms.[20] Paul would have found either sexual role, whether *malakos* or *arsenokoites,* as something distasteful and outside the bounds of appropriate community conduct.[21] Paul's understanding that the only purpose for sexual activity was for the creation of children is an overlay to this section. His writing and description of these vices, which included these sexual practices, would have given a nuance to, and reflected a strong scriptural Jewish condemnation of, sexual relationships between those of the same gender. This list of behaviors, which appears at the end of the condemnation of bringing lawsuits against fellow Christians, would have been a way for Paul to characterize those legal actions as equal to this other conduct that would have been considered outside the bounds of appropriate behavior for a community member.[22] This listing of behaviors also serves as a link between Paul's condemnation of the litigious nature of the community and what comes next in the remainder of chapter 6 and chapter 7: other issues of sexual morality and conduct, particularly in assigned roles, and an individual's conduct within a marriage.[23]

A goodly portion of the behaviors that Paul lists in 6:9–10 have as their focus greed and financial fraud: "thieves, robbers," people who are "greedy." Paul is including in the listing of sexual taboos other conduct that again links the prohibition against litigiousness with sexual conduct.[24] Paul is indicating that the community should not be involved with these kinds of activities. Paul concretizes this by saying the members of the community have been "washed" and "sanctified" and "justified" by being brought into the Christian community.[25] The listing of behaviors, in between an attack on litigious behavior and what Paul considers to be inappropriate sexual activity, highlights an important point. Although Paul has a predisposition against sexual practices between two males, the entirety of his focus is really an attack on any kind of sexual activity outside of marriage. To Paul, if sex is necessary at all, it should only occur in marriage and for procreation.[26]

These twelve verses at the beginning of chapter 6, regarding litigation and behaviors, serve as a segue between the conduct reviled in chapter 5 and the appropriate conduct within a marriage which follows in chapter 6. These bridge verses continue Paul's theme: a problem within the Corinthian church and its failure to actually be a church, a community.[27] By pointing to the problem of litigation and judgment, Paul is highlighting that the Corinthians were accommodating the culture around them, incorporating that culture's mores too much into their own, and losing sight of the things Paul directed them to keep in focus.[28] Paul is asking the Corinthians to think about their community's borders and how they relate to the world around them. He is asking that they differentiate themselves from that world surrounding them, and that they make and keep a distinctive culture that was all their own, modeled on the principles Paul set forth.[29]

Paul is trying to get the Corinthians to focus on a larger theological perspective in which to live. By his questions, Paul is focusing the community on changing and evaluating their practices and relationships among themselves. By focusing on litigation, he is highlighting a way they can practically change the way they interact. The byproduct Paul is hoping to achieve is a way to settle internal disputes that consolidate and strengthen the life of the internal community and the church, and consequently weaken the ties to the surrounding community.[30] By focusing the community on a different way of thinking, Paul is highlighting that wrongdoers will "not inherit the kingdom of God," as he says after providing his list of behaviors.[31]

Paul follows this list of vices with a series of quotations, which he counters with his own answers. In verse 12 he says twice, "All things are lawful for me." We can presume this is something the Corinthians have said to him. His response is, first, "but not all things are beneficial," and second, "but I will not be dominated by anything." By following the list of prohibited vices with this rhetorical device of making a statement and then challenging its basis, Paul is trying to change the attitudes expressed by the Corinthians.[32] Paul is focusing their attention on the importance of the body itself—the individual body and how that body is used in relation to each other and God. These illustrative vices that take place just before this mock argument Paul sets up are exemplifiers not of new rules for sexual behavior, but to criticize the Corinthians for taking each other to court as opposed to resolving disputes within the community. The vices listed are simply illustrative of how the Corinthians were before Paul established the community and the church to which they now belong; he is instructing them not to revert to them.[33]

These lists of vices in 6:9–10 expands the two lists of vices Paul provided in chapter 5, adding what Paul considered sexual misconduct: adultery, pederasty, and sex between males.[34] Paul uses this expanded list of vices to create a cumulative effect on the reader. In chapter 5 Paul focuses on the immoral, the greedy, robbers, idolaters, revilers, and drunkards, as found in 5:10–11. In chapter 6 Paul adds four more: adulterers, effeminates, males who sleep with males, and thieves. Although Paul disapproves of these kinds of conduct, Paul is leading up to a discussion of appropriate sexual behavior and marriage obligations. He is saying, "You were like that, but now you are not." The Corinthians have been changed by their baptism into this new church community founded on Paul's understanding of the world. This cumulative building of the behaviors was meant to accentuate their difference to the world around them, as well as to the way "they were before."[35]

The vice lists assist Paul in distinguishing acceptable behavior for community members and allowing those community members to become properly identifiable believers.[36] His emphasis on the court system makes these distinguishing characteristics more concrete for his readers. The court system was Roman in origin and had a strong bias in favor of the upper and wealthier classes, like most other things in that society. The clear majority of litigation involved wealthy and powerful people fighting against people of lesser status. Many of these disputes focused on the taking of property from those in the lower strata of society, with the resultant amassing of wealth by those in the upper echelon. This "taking" by the wealthy, this focus on the care of the privileged and the bias against those not as privileged is an example of greed that Paul would have found intolerable.[37]

In a similar fashion, Paul would have found the sexual abuse of slaves and those of the lower classes as abhorrent. Right after this list of vices, Paul focuses on the importance of keeping the body pure, of not denigrating the body by acts he believed to be worthless and debasing of the gift of Jesus's sacrifice of his body on the Cross. Paul uses this list of vices as a vehicle to exhibit a sharp contrast to the exalted position the body holds for Paul, who believed in the bodily resurrection of not only Jesus but of each believer as well.[38] As repugnant as it is to our understanding, sexual relations between a man and a young boy was not thought of as wrong by the surrounding community, but was in fact an activity looked upon in Greek circles as part of the culture of educated adults. Paul, as well as the Jewish and Christian communities to whom he was writing, would not have looked upon that activity as appropriate.[39]

Paul uses these lists of behaviors to illustrate why litigation is inappropriate between people living in Christian community. It is a misuse of this passage to focus on this list of behaviors as Paul's main point. It is placing an incorrect emphasis on these behaviors. The focus is Paul's insistence that the Corinthians act as a community. The use of litigation to settle disputes is inappropriate and interferes with the community acting like a Christian community. Paul highlights this point of the need for the community to act like a community by saying they have been transformed by their baptism into something new, into something different than that which surrounds them.[40] He ends the list of behaviors by saying just as they were like that before, they are no longer. At the end of verse 11 Paul uses the word *alla* three times: "*alla apolouo, alla habiazo, alla dikaioo*." A literal translation would be, "But you were washed, but you were sanctified, but you were justified." Not all translations provide the "but" before each action. By not doing so, they lessen the power of Paul's argument. The word *alla*, "but," is one of the strongest Greek words used to emphasis contrast.[41] Paul is illustrating for the Corinthians what their former life was like and how they are now different: how they have been "washed, sanctified, and justified" in their baptism. Paul is saying "you were like this, but you were washed, but you were sanctified, but you were justified." One can almost hear Paul raising his voice and shaking his finger at the Corinthians. They should not be suing one another; they should know better and should be acting in a more appropriate fashion.

Although Paul's list of behaviors includes reference to not only the passive person in a same gender relationship but also the active one, the kinds of sexual relationships to which Paul is referring are vastly different than how we understand sexuality between queer partners today. Not only would we view the kind of activity to which Paul is referring as anathema today, it is hard not to be appalled at the idea of men utilizing boys for sexual pleasure, or men utilizing adult slaves, or adult males from a lower class, to satisfy a sexual urge where consent was not even an afterthought. There is no concept of mutuality, or love, or monogamy in what Paul is describing. It is about power and violence, and the satisfaction of sexual desire by any available manner. The type and kind of queer relationship that is mutual, loving, and entered freely based upon respect and love is not Paul's focus, or a part of his consciousness or worldview. This passage, and the list of behaviors that illustrate a mindset of cruelty and abuse, cannot be utilized, in all good conscience, as against queer relationships as they exist and are understood.

CHAPTER FIVE

1 Timothy 1

Paul, an apostle of Christ Jesus by the command of God our
Savior and of Christ Jesus our hope, [2] To Timothy, my loyal
child in the faith: Grace, mercy, and peace from God the
Father and Christ Jesus our Lord. [3] I urge you, as I did when
I was on my way to Macedonia, to remain in Ephesus so that
you may instruct certain people not to teach any different
doctrine, [4] and not to occupy themselves with myths and
endless genealogies that promote speculations rather than
the divine training that is known by faith. [5] But the aim of
such instruction is love that comes from a pure heart, a good
conscience, and sincere faith. [6] Some people have deviated
from these and turned to meaningless talk, [7] desiring to be
teachers of the law, without understanding either what they
are saying or the things about which they make assertions.
[8] Now we know that the law is good, if one uses it legitimately.
[9] This means understanding that the law is laid down not for
the innocent but for the lawless and disobedient, for the
godless and sinful, for the unholy and profane, for those
who kill their father or mother, for murderers, [10] fornicators,
sodomites, slave traders, liars, perjurers, and whatever else

is contrary to the sound teaching 11 that conforms to the
glorious gospel of the blessed God, which he entrusted to me.
12 I am grateful to Christ Jesus our Lord, who has strength-
ened me, because he judged me faithful and appointed me
to his service, 13 even though I was formerly a blasphemer,
a persecutor, and a man of violence. But I received mercy
because I had acted ignorantly in unbelief, 14 and the grace
of our Lord overflowed for me with the faith and love that
are in Christ Jesus. 15 The saying is sure and worthy of full
acceptance, that Christ Jesus came into the world to save
sinners—of whom I am the foremost. 16 But for that very
reason I received mercy, so that in me, as the foremost,
Jesus Christ might display the utmost patience, making me
an example to those who would come to believe in him for
eternal life. 17 To the King of the ages, immortal, invisible, the
only God, be honor and glory forever and ever. Amen. 18 I am
giving you these instructions, Timothy, my child, in accordance with the prophecies made earlier about you, so that by
following them you may fight the good fight, 19 having faith
and a good conscience. By rejecting conscience, certain
persons have suffered shipwreck in the faith; 20 among them
are Hymenaeus and Alexander, whom I have turned over to
Satan, so that they may learn not to blaspheme.

1 Timothy is the first of the Pastoral Epistles—1 Timothy, 2 Timothy, and Titus—called that because there are many instructions within them addressed to pastors of congregations.[1] These letters, whose authorship is disputed, do not have any indication of cross-knowledge between them. There is also no indication that would allow us to know which of these was written first. The

letter entitled 1 Timothy is the longest and has consequently been given preeminence.[2]

Since the beginning of the nineteenth century, scholars have disputed the authorship of these letters. The debate rages on today and will not be repeated here, save for the understanding that it will be presumed for the purposes of this writing that this letter was not written by Paul. Many posit that this letter was written after Paul's death by an individual who was devoted to Paul and wanted to continue Paul's authoritarian voice to the communities he had founded.[3]

By the end of the first century, and after his death, Paul had been given a significant and almost mythic position in the church, with different groups and people competing to guard the truth as espoused by Paul. It is with little wonder that a devoted adherent, following the tradition of that time, would utilize a well-renowned name to write a letter and to continue teaching and forming the existing Christian communities according to the author's understanding of Pauline tradition.[4]

The structure of 1 Timothy is different from letters that have no questions about Paul being the author. The overall structure can be broken down into: instructions to Timothy to stay in Ephesus and combat false teaching (1:1–11); a recitation of Paul's commissioning (1:12–20); a discussion on prayer in church (2:1–15); a discussion on bishops and deacons (3:1–13); a discussion on heresy and the end times (4:1–16); a review of appropriate behavior of community members (5:1–6.2); issuance of further warnings against false teachers (6:3–21).[5] The portion of the letter which is the focus of this study, 1:1–11, falls at the very beginning of this correspondence.

After the author's initial greeting, he jumps right into one of the main topics: concern about incorrect teachings. The author is saying the recipients of the letter are allowing topics of little import to occupy the time and attention of members of the community.[6] The topics addressed in this letter are arranged in an alternating fashion: contrasting true and false teachers with other instructions for church governance, and the appropriate behavior of community members.[7] The author splits chapter 1 into four distinct subsections, with the verses under study here (verses 8–11) being the second of the four.[8] Surrounding verses 8–11 the author sets out the heresy to which he is objecting. This heresy has two flaws: the law is misused, and there is a misunderstanding of how great a role God's grace and mercy play in an individual's salvation.[9] This understanding brackets the behaviors listed in the verses under review. Although the behaviors in 1:8–11 may appear to be a digression from the purpose of the letter, they are not. They are actually the literary device used to set up the rest of the teachings and instructions.[10]

Just prior to 1:8–11 the author criticizes the "new" teachers, contrasting their meaningless talk of genealogies and myths, and their misuse of "the law," as misleading regarding the true faith found in Paul's teachings.[11] The author wants Timothy and the community to oppose false teachers and to be examples for all members of the community of believers by doing so.[12] According to 1 Timothy 1:8–9, the law's only purpose is to restrain the lawless, underpinning one of the main points of the letter: that sound teaching and proper behavior are integrally intertwined.[13]

There is a presumption that "the law" to which the author is referring is the law found in the Torah. This presumption is based on the organization of the list of behaviors which follow the author's statement, and roughly mimic the Hebrew Testament's Decalogue. After the list of behaviors, the author references the gospel of Jesus and the salvation of sinners provided through the grace of Jesus. This indicates that "the law" is not this gospel but something else, leading to the conclusion that the law is found in the Torah.[14] Even though "the law" has been overtaken by the Gospels, the author is not saying that the law does not have a continuing purpose. The author speaks confidently and positively about the law as being "sound doctrine" and serves the purpose of pointing people to appropriate behavior.[15]

These individuals whom the author may have been attacking were people who wanted to teach the Jewish law without understanding that its true meaning and purpose were to change the behavior of lawless individuals.[16] The author of 1 Timothy agrees that the law only applies to those who are living in an unrighteous fashion, and it does not apply to those who follow the gospel because they are already living a righteous life.[17] The people the author of 1 Timothy is attacking were trying to apply the Mosaic law to all people. The author is saying that the law is only for those who are opposed to—or do not yet know—the teachings of the gospel.[18]

As we have seen in other chapters of this study, translation issues play an important role in deciphering the meaning and intent of the author, the passage, and the letter itself. This is true for 1 Timothy. The verses in question have been translated in different ways (emphasis added):

NRSV: 9 This means understanding that the law is laid down not for the innocent but for the lawless and disobedient, for the godless and sinful, for the unholy and profane, for those who kill their father or mother, for murderers, 10 *fornicators, sodomites, slave traders,* liars, perjurers, and whatever else is contrary to the sound teaching 11 that conforms to the glorious gospel of the blessed God, which he entrusted to me.

NASB: 8 But we know that the Law is good, if one uses it lawfully, 9 realizing the fact that law is not made for a righteous person, but for those who are lawless and rebellious, for the ungodly and sinners, for the unholy and worldly, for those who kill their fathers or mothers, for murderers 10 *for the sexually immoral, homosexuals, slave traders,* liars, perjurers, and whatever else is contrary to sound teaching, 11 according to the glorious gospel of the blessed God, with which I have been entrusted.

ESV: 8 Now we know that the law is good, if one uses it lawfully, 9 understanding this, that the law is not laid down for the just but for the lawless and disobedient, for the ungodly and sinners, for the unholy and profane, for those who strike their fathers and mothers, for murderers, [10] *the sexually immoral, men who practice homosexuality, enslavers,* liars, perjurers, and whatever else is contrary to sound doctrine, [11] in accordance with the glorious gospel of the blessed God with which I have been entrusted.

KJV: [8] But we know that the law is good, if a man use it lawfully; [9] Knowing this, that the law is not made for a righteous man, but for the lawless and disobedient, for the ungodly and for sinners, for unholy and profane, for murderers of fathers and murderers of mothers, for manslayers, [10] *For whoremongers, for them that defile themselves with mankind, for menstealers*, for liars, for perjured persons, and if there be any other thing that is contrary to sound doctrine; [11] According to the glorious gospel of the blessed God, which was committed to my trust.

NIV: [8] We know that the law is good if one uses it properly. [9] We also know that law {9 Or that the law} is made not for the righteous but for lawbreakers and rebels, the ungodly and sinful, the unholy and irreligious; for those who kill their fathers or mothers, for murderers, [10] *for adulterers and perverts, for slave traders* and liars and perjurers—and for whatever else is contrary to the sound doctrine [11] that conforms to the glorious gospel of the blessed God, which he entrusted to me.

The Greek words translated are *pornos arsenokoites andrapodistes*. These five translations translate them differently, each with a different connotation. It is important to understand these words as they would have been understood by the original readers, and then apply that understanding to the text as it was written. After that review, an analysis should be undertaken that brings an understanding of these words and this text forward to our time.[19]

The first word, *pornos,* is a dative masculine plural noun that literally means "a fornicator, an immoral person."[20] The word has been translated five different ways in the examples provided: fornicators, immoral men, sexually immoral, whoremongers, adulterers. Each of these words have their own nuance and can slant the text's meaning in a direction. In the Pastoral Epistles, this is the only place *pornos* or its cognates occur.[21] As *pornos* is a masculine plural noun, the author is likely referring to an immoral person, or fornicator, who is either a male prostitute or a man having sex outside of marriage. As the author of 1 Timothy shows heavy disdain for women later in the letter, the choice of the masculine plural of the noun is no accident.[22] The author is pointing to a male having sex outside the confines of the marriage bed.[23] This sexually active male would have been considered "sexually immoral." To attempt to define the offending sexual acts further is impossible, as the word *pornos* is a general phrase used to describe a person who commits adultery: literally, sexual activity outside of marriage.[24]

The second word *arsenokoites* is also a dative masculine plural noun. In the five translations cited, the word has been translated as: sodomites, homosexuals, men who practice homosexuality, them that defile themselves with mankind, perverts. Each of these translations, like the word before it, has its own nuance, thereby giving the translation a different understanding. *Arsenokoites* is a compound word made up of *arseno,* which means "male," and *koites,* which literally means "bed," with connotations of "marriage bed."[25] Substantive discussion revolves around this word, some of which was reviewed in the preceding chapter on 1 Corinthians 6, where a cognate of this word is utilized. The connotations of this word and the idea of a "marriage bed" harken back to the discussion on Leviticus 18 and 20, and would indicate a dominant male who takes a compliant male to bed for the purposes of sex, the compliant male "acting in the role of a woman."[26]

As has been discussed previously, the culture that existed in the area to which the author was writing was one where much of the sexual activity taking place was about power. Mutuality as we understand the term today was not a part of that culture.

It is likely that the author was referring to an adult male who was having sex with either a younger male, or an individual from a lower class, or male slave. There has been argument that this word applies to all those who "practice homosexuality."[27] To define *arsenokoites* as those who "practice homosexuality" is to apply an incorrect nuance and connotation. It is incorrect to call the kind of abusive activity of either an adult male having sexual relations with a younger boy, or with a person who had no choice in the matter (such as someone from a lower class, or a slave) as homosexuality or representative of queer culture. These kinds of relationships were not based in mutual love, understanding, and compassion, but were a taking, a using of someone else, for one's own sexual gratification.

This passage is not about queer culture as we understand it today. The passage and this list of behaviors are the author's attempt to point to behavior that would require those individuals to pay attention to the law, which according to this author is intended to be a guide to people who transgress sexual fidelity in relationships, along with those who are maternal and paternal murderers, liars, and slave traders.[28] This passage is focused on false teachers, with the reference to *pornos* (sexually immoral males) and *arsenokoites* (males who lie in bed with males as with females) as examples of people for whom the law was intended. These references are not the focus of this passage, or of this letter, but are merely examples of individuals who are in violation of "the law."[29]

The author writes to a community instructing them to hold fast to what was considered true Pauline teaching.[30] The author reflects his opinions of what the ideal Christian would act and be like. By listing these proscriptions, the author provides evidence to us that there were groups of Christians who did not define sex, gender, and age categories as the letter defines them. These lists provide further evidence that there were multiple groups of Christians with wide and varied beliefs and practices they believed to be acceptable.[31] This is an important concept to grasp, as it provides insight into the life of the churches at the end of the first century and the beginning of the second.[32] It appears from the nuances of this letter that the people interpreting Paul's teachings in Timothy's community were the individuals that the author of 1 Timothy found objectionable. The author uses Paul's name as a tool to influence the recipients of the letter to change their behaviors.[33]

First Timothy's list of behaviors contains serious, extreme, and unusual crimes: paternal and maternal murder, people who lie, the godless, the profane. This list of behaviors is different from other lists, as it personalizes the moral misconduct.[34] The letter leads to an understanding that the correction being demanded is an adherence to the law, leading the individual to open their eyes to God's mercy.[35]

The focus of 1 Timothy may have less to do with conflicts within the internal churches themselves, which was the focus of many of the letters attributed to Paul. First Timothy is more focused on social problems and the customs of patronage and wealth, both of which influenced the individual churches, coming from those outside the community.[36] It is likely the author was advising a newly developing heresy referred to as Gnosticism. The derivation of the word "Gnosticism" helps to define it. It comes from the Greek word for knowledge: *gnosis*. Gnosticism espoused that knowledge of God was attainable by only a few. It was a revealed knowledge of God and of the origin of humanity, and would lead to an understanding of the spiritual part of humanity through which one could receive redemption. This secret knowledge was established in the Apostles and passed down through a secret tradition.[37] Gnostics degraded the created world and the human body, calling individuals to an ascetic life. They also called on their followers to be part of a radically individualistic spiritualism, discarding the belief of the Church as the body of Christ.[38]

The time in which 1 Timothy was written was different from ours in culture and worldview. The early church was still struggling to develop, with multiple competing interests inside and outside of the budding institution, many in conflict. The highly stratified and paternalistic society led to abuse of human beings. Understanding that fact when making sense of scriptural texts like 1 Timothy is important in placing these writings in context.

This passage is not a condemnation of queer people in the twenty-first century, but is a further example of a condemnation of a type of behavior queer people, as well as any civilized individual today, would condemn: violence, rape, the unwanted sexual taking of another person. These behaviors and actions can in no way be applied to queer people. The behaviors which are included on 1 Timothy's list are ones emblematic of a stratified, paternalistic society where power, sex, and one's station in life were intricately intertwined. This passage has nothing to do with a mutually agreed upon, loving relationship between adults. To use it as such is a misuse of the text and perpetuates unneeded harm.

CONCLUSION

Although the seven passages of this study from six books in the Bible were written at different times throughout history, a common thread runs through all of them. They all focus on the violent and wrongful taking and misuse of another individual. In Genesis, the story of Sodom and Gomorrah comes in the middle of the Abraham saga, part of which provides the reader with a model for righteous and God-focused living. The threat of violent rape and unwanted taking of first the angels, and then Lot's daughter, have nothing to do with sexual relations. Rape, or attempted rape, is not sex. Rape is a cruel violation of another human being, a wrongful taking of that person. The story in Genesis is not about sex or "homosexuality." The focus of this story is power and the misuse of it, and cannot be used as a condemnation of queer people.

The same can be said for the story of the unnamed concubine in Judges. Her brutal rape, caused by her taking the place of her husband when he pushes her out to a crowd standing at the door, is an example of the depth of human depravity. Once again, this story is not about sex or "homosexuality"; it is about the abuse of power by a people who have fallen away from a right relationship with God.

The laws and rules set forth in Leviticus were written to provide Israel with a way to be distinct and separate from the culture that surrounded them. The Israelite people were about to enter the Promised Land. The laws were meant to assist Israel in growing into a strong and populous nation. The laws were created to bring the holiness that was part of the priest cult and the temple to the whole population of Israel. Part of those laws and rules, created by a remnant of the priest cult while in exile, had to do with sexual activity. This highly structured and stratified patriarchal society that is reflected in Leviticus would have found it difficult to accept anyone who did not fit into this rigidly maintained hierarchal structure. Women were considered property, with one of their major duties to bear children. They were used for this purpose. For a man to not participate in this kind of procreative activity and "to lie down in the place of lying" did not fit the structure of society Leviticus was attempting to implement.[1] In fact, that patriarchal structure would be threatened by anyone not following these laws and rules established to try and build a society and protect that fledgling society and culture.

Paul's letter to the Romans is not condemning "homosexuality." It is focused on appropriate relationship with God, a central tenet of which is the proper worship of God. The letter is a strong condemnation of idol worship and the inappropriate "use" or "utilization" of another. This kind of "use" or "utilization" is equivalent to a wrongful taking of another's humanity: a violation of their God-given right to not be abused. Appropriate living, proper treatment of another, are things Paul is calling for in Romans. This passage has nothing to do with a mutual and loving relationship between two people of the same gender. Paul is focused on the inappropriate sexual taking and use of another person.

These same issues arise in Paul's first letter to the Corinthians. Here we see Paul insisting on the Corinthian Christians being distinct from the culture around them, and treating each other with respect. Paul is focusing on wrongful taking: the wrongful taking of property in litigation, the wrongful taking of another human being's dignity. Paul refers to prostitutes and the licentious ways of people who are not living out a loving and mutually respectful relationship in community. The behaviors he lists and condemns are the inappropriate use, utilization, and taking of another's humanity. There was no mutuality, no respect involved in these relationships. Power, violence, and selfish gratification are the focus of Paul's condemnation. The people Paul refers to are not "homosexuals" as we understand that term in the twenty-first century, but are people abusing and using others for their own sexual gratification. These same arguments apply to 1 Timothy. Queer people in the twenty-first century are not the target or focus of Paul's attention.

The rhetorical literary devices Paul and his followers utilized to cite the heinous abuse of human beings in a societal and cultural setting, based in what the twenty-first century would term patriarchy, misogyny, slavery, and sexual abuse, cannot be used as an example of God's displeasure toward queer people.

Passages that condemn these kinds of conduct, these kinds of abuses, do not marginalize people who are in loving, committed, and mutual relationships. These passages do not apply to them. The living and breathing words of God that live in these pages argue for a radical and complete love of all people, the inclusion of all people, and a protection of those who are abused, used, utilized, and taken by those who have real or perceived power over them.

This study has highlighted the variables in language associated with translation. It is vital to know what translation is being utilized when these, or any passage, in the Bible are under review or discussion. Nuances, societal structures of the communities for whom the texts were originally intended, and anthropological data concerning those societies are all factors that need to be added to the mix in understanding these words that can carry so much weight and authority with them. Having knowledge and words to counter baseless accusations can disarm those who would use these passages as weapons of exclusion and judgement, and can empower the queer community to live confidently in God's love.

The Bible is God's living word to us. Just as God is not finished with us yet, so our understanding of the Bible in not finished. All of God's human creation are children of God and deserve the opportunity to read, struggle with, and seek a deeper relationship with God through those interactions. The texts of this study should not be an impediment to the deepening of that relationship, but in fact a vehicle toward a greater understanding of God's deep and abiding love for all of us.

ENDNOTES

Chapter One

1. Boadt, 375.
2. Wenham, *Genesis 16–50*, 62.
3. Wenham, *Genesis 16–50,* 64.
4. Fretherm, 474.
5. Wenham, "Genesis," *Eerdmans Commentary*, 53.
6. Boadt, 376.
7. DeGroot, 22.
8. See: Fretherm, 473–74; Whybray, 52; Kselman, 94; Wenham, "Genesis," *Eerdmans Commentary*, 53; Boadt, 375; Wenham, "Genesis," *New Bible Commentary,* 74; Dahlberg, 108; Wenham, *Genesis 16–50,* 63.
9. See *The Navarre Bible: The Petateuch*, 108. This Roman Catholic tradition goes down the road of homosexuality being the motivating factor in God's wrath.
10. Wenham, *Genesis 16–50,* 63–64.
11. The references are: Isa. 1:9; Isa. 13:19; Jer. 23:14; Jer. 49:18; Amos 4:11; Zeph. 2:9; Ezek. 16:46; Deut. 29:23; Deut. 32:32.
12. Exum, 223.
13. Fewell, 73.
14. Mafico, 564.
15. Judges 19:1.
16. Exum, 223.

17. Kwasi, 76.
18. Olsen, 872.
19. Niditch, 189.
20. Ibid., 176.
21. Fewell, 73.
22. Deut. 31:12.
23. Exum, 237.
24. Fewell, 81.
25. Olson, 876, and Genesis 34:3.
26. Fewell, 83.
27. Guest, 203.
28. Exum, 238.
29. Fewell, 83.
30. Eves, 143.
31. Webb, 282, and Deut.16:14, 26:12.
32. See Exod. 22:21, 23:9; Lev. 19:33–34; Deut. 10:18–19; and Olson, 876.
33. Webb, 283.
34. See: Olsen, 877; Guest, 293; Mafico, 564; Kwasi, 78; Webb, 283; Fewell, 81; Exum, 237.
35. Eves, 143.
36. Niditch, 189.
37. Mafico, 563.
38. Exum, 225.
39. Mafico, 562–63.
40. Guest, 204.
41. Olson, 878–79.
42. Williams, 7, 31, 37
43. Ibid., 211–15.
44. Ibid., 18.
45. Matt. 22:37–39; see also Mark 12:30–32 and Luke 10:27–29.

Chapter Two

1. Pigott, 51.
2. Cross and Livingstone, 1261.

3. Levoratti, 448–49.
4. Cooper and Scholz, 31.
5. See: Levoratti, 453, and Kaiser, 997.
6. See Kaiser, 986–87, and Cooper and Scholz, 39.
7. Cooper and Scholz, 33.
8. Houston, 102.
9. Kaiser, 989.
10. Cooper and Scholz, 39.
11. Wright, 122.
12. Pigott, 66.
13. Ibid., 50–52.
14. Houston, 116.
15. Ibid.
16. Gorman, 160.
17. Watts, 170.
18. Kaiser, 1125.
19. Grabbe, 102
20. Ibid.
21. Haynes, 23–27.
22. Brueggemann, 90.
23. Ibid., 92.
24. Ibid.
25. Fox, 598.
26. Ibid., 599.
27. See: Gen. 49:4, Job 7:13, Prov. 7:17, Song of Sol. 3:1, Daniel 4:2, 4:7, 4:10.
28. My translation.
29. Gorman, 160.
30. *Navarre*, 418.
31. Hartley, 298–99.
32. Levoratti, 447.
33. Ibid., 448.
34. Houston, 116.
35. Wright, 146.
36. Kaiser, 1125.
37. Houston, 102.
38. Kaiser, 1124, and Houston, 101.

39. Wegner, 242–43.
40. Cooper and Scholz, 38.
41. Pigott, 51.
42. Cooper and Scholz, 37.
43. Kaiser, 988.
44. Levoratti, 447, and Wright, 145.
45. Wright, 122.
46. Kaiser, 1127.
47. See Leviticus verses: 18:26, 27, 29, 30 and 20:25.
48. As examples, see Hartley, 341, Levoratti, 470, Newsom and Ringe, 44.
49. Pigott, 52.
50. Watts, 171.
51. Kaiser, 1141.
52. Wright, 149.
53. Watts, 171.
54. Cross and Livingstone, 1261.
55. Cooper and Scholz, 38.
56. Houston, 118.
57. Kaiser, 1142.
58. Gorman, 146.
59. Pigott, 52.
60. Houston, 116–18.
61. Cooper and Scholz, 38–39.
62. Brown, 30.
63. See Lev. 19:19 and Deut. 22:9–11.

Chapter Three

1. "The Future of the Anglican Communion and ECUSA: A Communion in Crisis," forum presentation by Lord Carey at Virginia Theological Seminary on March 12, 2006.
2. See: Achtemeir, 8; Byrne, 1–2; *New Oxford Annotated Bible*, 242NT; Dunn, 71; Meyer, 1042; Jewett, *Romans*, 165; P. Brown, 564 as commentators agreeing with this point.

3. Metzger, 446–47.
4. See P. Brown, 565; Hill, 1088; and Meyer, 1042, for a more detailed discussion.
5. P. Brown, 560.
6. Dunn, 70.
7. See: Meyer, 1043; Byrne, 4; Hill, 1083–84; Jewett, *Romans*, 41–42.
8. Meyer, 1042; and Hill, 1088.
9. Byrne, 8; Jewett, *Romans*, 41–42.
10. Byrne, 18–19.
11. Ibid., 63.
12. Meyer, 1043.
13. Jewett, *Romans*, 165.
14. Ibid.
15. Schreiner, 91.
16. For a sampling of these texts see: Gen. 14:20; Exod. 21:13; Num. 21:3; Deut. 2:33; Josh. 2:24; Judges 16:23; 1 Sam. 14:12; 2 Chron. 13:16; Job 16:11; Isa. 53:6; Dan. 2:38.
17. Meyer, 1043.
18. Hill, 1086.
19. Ibid.
20. Kykkotis, 660.
21. See: 1 Sam. 1:28; 2 Kings 1:13; Rom. 1:26, 27; Wisd. of Sol. 15:7; Wisd. of Sol. 15:15; Sir. 18:9.
22. See white paper delivered by The Rev. Grey Temple, "The Biblical Case in Favor of Gene Robinson's Election, Confirmation and Consecration," given at Holy Innocents Church, Atlanta, GA, September 11, 2003.
23. Bromiley, 9:772.
24. Jewett, *Romans*, 175–76.
25. Temple, "Biblical Case."
26. Hill, 1090.
27. Schreiner, 91–92.
28. Dunn, 72.
29. Jewett, *Romans*, 173.
30. Ibid., 178.

31. Byrne, 66.
32. Hawtorne, Martin, and Reid, 414.
33. Gaventa, 407; Meyer, 1044; Achtemeier, 38–39.
34. Byrne, 68.
35. Jewett, *Romans*, 163.
36. Ibid., 179.
37. Achteimeier, 40.
38. Ibid., 41.
39. Byrne, 65, 70.
40. Hill, 1090.
41. Schreiner, 91.
42. Byrne, 4.
43. Schreiner, 94–96.
44. Byrne, 69.
45. Ibid., 70.
46. Ibid., 65.
47. Jewett, *Romans*, 176.
48. Ibid., 42, 173.
49. Ibid., 180.
50. Ibid., 181.
51. Meyer, 1044.
52. Jewett, *Romans*, 46–58.

Chapter Four

1. NRSV, 267 NT.
2. R. E Brown, 512.
3. Fiorenza, 1080.
4. Barclay, 1116.
5. Fiorenza, 1080.
6. Hays, 92.
7. Collins, 225.
8. Lambrecht, 1609.

9. Ibid., 1611.
10. Hays, 99.
11. P. Brown, 560.
12. Hays, 97.
13. Collins, 230, 236.
14. Sampley, 858.
15. Hays, 97.
16. Barclay, 1117.
17. Ibid.
18. Sampley, 859.
19. Hays, 102.
20. Conzelmann, 106.
21. Barclay, 1117.
22. Barton, 1326.
23. Collins, 230.
24. Barclay, 1117.
25. Ibid.
26. P. Brown, 530.
27. Hays, 93.
28. Barclay, 1110.
29. Sampley, 855.
30. Barton, 1326.
31. Lambrecht, 1611.
32. Hays, 102.
33. Ibid., 97.
34. Collins, 225.
35. Fiorenza, 1081.
36. Sampley, 855.
37. Hays, 93.
38. Barton, 1327.
39. P. Brown, 529.
40. Hays, 98.
41. Sampley, 855.

Chapter Five

1. Dewey, 444.
2. R. E. Brown, 653.
3. Hultgren, 144.
4. Drury, 1220.
5. See Dewey, 446, R. E. Brown, 654, Hultgren, 149–50 for a more comprehensive breakdown.
6. Bassler, 1138.
7. NRSV, NT350. Warning about false teachings are located at 1:3–2:15; 4:1–5:2; 6:2–21, while instructions regarding behavior and church governance are located at 3:1–16, 5:3–6:1, thereby showing the alternating pattern within the letter.
8. Mounce, 30.
9. Ibid.
10. See Bassler, 1138, and Mounce, 30.
11. Bassler, 1138.
12. Hultgren, 149.
13. Bassler, 1138.
14. NRSV, NT351.
15. Guthrie, 1295–96.
16. Drury, 1222.
17. Mounce, 30.
18. Ibid., 44.
19. Dibelius and Conzelmann, 24.
20. P. Brown, 645.
21. Mounce, 38.
22. Dewey, 444–45.
23. Mounce, 38.
24. Towner, 127.
25. Mounce, 38–39.
26. See pages 32–34, and 41–44 of this study.
27. Towner, 127.
28. Oden, 39.
29. P. Brown, 659–60.

30. Drury, 1220.
31. Dewey, 445.
32. Perkins, 1430.
33. Bassler, 1137.
34. Towner, 124.
35. Oden, 38.
36. Perkins, 1429.
37. Cross and Livingstone, 687.
38. Hultgren, 153.

Conclusion

1. See pages 32–34, and 41–44 of this study for more detailed discussion of this point.

BIBLIOGRAPHY

General Reference to All Chapters

Bromiley, Geoffrey W. *Theological Dictionary of the New Testament*. Abridged in One Volume. Edited by Gerhard Kittel and Gerhard Friedrich. Grand Rapids, MI: Wm Eerdmans, 1985.

Brown, Peter. *The Body and Society: Men, Women and Sexual Renunciation in Early Christianity.* New York: Columbia University Press, 1988.

Brown, Raymond E. *An Introduction to the New Testament.* New York: Doubleday, 1996.

Coogan, M. D. *The New Oxford Annotated Bible with Apocrypha: New Revised Standard Version.* 3rd ed. New York: Oxford University Press, 2001.

Cross, F. L., and E. A. Livingstone, eds. *The Oxford Dictionary of the Christian Church.* 3rd rev. ed. New York: Oxford University Press, 2005.

Dode, L. *The History of Homosexuality.* Toronto, Canada: Arete Publishing, 2004.

Hawthorne, Gerald F., Ralph P. Martin, and Daniel G. Reid, eds. *Dictionary of Paul and His Letters*. Downers Grove, IL: InterVarsity Press, 1993.

Kittel, Gerhard, and Gerhard Friedrich, eds. *Theological Dictionary of the New Testament*. Vol. 5. Translated by Geoffrey W. Bromiley. Grand Rapids, MI: Wm Eerdmans, 1967.

———. *Theological Dictionary of the New Testament.* Vol. 9. Translated by Geoffrey W. Bromiley. Grand Rapids, MI: Wm Eerdmans, 1974.

Kykkotis, I. *English-Greek & Greek-English Dictionary.* London: Lund Humphries & Co., 1942,

Levenson, J. D. *Sinai and Zion: An Entry Into the Jewish Bible.* New York: Harper & Row 1987.

Metzger, Bruce M. *A Textual Commentary on the Greek New Testament*. 2nd ed. Stuttgart, Germany: United Bible Societies, 1994.

Moulton, J. H., and G. Milligan. *The Vocabulary of the Greek New Testament.* Grand Rapids, MI: Wm B. Eerdmans, 1949.

The Navarre Bible: The Pentateuch. Princeton, NJ: Scepter Publishers, 1996.

Tucker, G. M. *Form Criticism of the Old Testament.* Philadelphia, PA: Fortress Press, 1971.

Williams, C. A. *Roman Homosexuality.* Oxford: Oxford University Press, 1999.

Works Utilized for Genesis

Boadt, L. "Genesis." In *The International Bible Commentary: A Catholic and Ecumenical Commentary for the Twenty-First Century,* edited by William R. Farmer. Minneapolis, MN: Liturgical Press, 1998.

Dahlberg, B. T. "Genesis." In *Mercer Commentary on the Bible*, edited by Watson E. Mills and Richard F. Wilson. Macon, GA: Mercer University Press, 1995.

DeGroot, Christiana. "Genesis." In *The IVP Women's Bible Commentary*, edited by Catherine Clark Kroeger and Mary J. Evans. Downer's Grove, IL: InterVasity Press, 2002.

Fretherm, T. E. "Genesis." In *The New Interpreter's Bible.* Vol. 1, edited by Walter Brueggemann, Walter C. Kaiser, Leander E. Keck, and Terence E. Fretheim. Nashville, TN: Abingdon Press, 1994.

Kselman, J. S. "Genesis." In *The Harper Collins Bible Commentary*, edited by James L. Mays. New York: Harper San Francisco, 2000.

Niditch, Sharon. "Genesis." In *Women's Bible Commentary*, edited by Carol A. Newson and Sharon H. Ringe. Louisville, KY: Westminster John Knox Press, 1998.

Wenham, Gordan J. "Genesis." In *New Bible Commentary*, edited by G. J. Wenham, J. A. Motyer, D. A. Carson, and R. T. France. 21st century ed. Downer's Grove, IL: InterVarsity Press, 1994.

———. "Genesis." In *Eerdmans Commentary on the Bible*, edited by James D. G. Dunn, and John W. Rogerson. Grand Rapids, MI: William B. Eerdmans, 2003.

———. *Genesis 16–50.* Vol. 2 of *Word Biblical Commentary.* Waco, TX: Word Books, 1994.

Whybray, R. H. "Genesis." In *The Oxford Bible Commentary*, edited by John Barton and John Muddiman. New York: Oxford University Press, 2001.

Works Utilized for Judges

Eves, Ailish Fergus. "Judges." In *The IVP Women's Bible Commentary*, edited by Catherine Clark Kroeger and Mary J. Evans. Downer's Grove, IL: InterVasity Press, 2002.

Exum, J. C. "Judges." In *The Harper Collins Bible Commentary*, edited by James L. Mays. New York: Harper San Francisco, 2000.

Fewell, Danna Nolan. "Judges." In *Women's Bible Commentary*, edited by Carol A. Newson and Sharon H. Ringe. Louisville, KY: Westminster John Knox Press, 1998.

Guest, P. Deryn. "Judges." In *Eerdmans Commentary on the Bible,* edited by James D. G. Dunn, and John W. Rogerson. Grand Rapids, MI: William B. Eerdmans, 2003.

Kwasi, F. U. "Judges." In *Global Bible Commentary*, edited by Daniel Patte. Nashville, TN: Abingdon Press, 2004.

Mafico, Temba L. J. "Judges." In *The International Bible Commentary: A Catholic and Ecumenical Commentary for the Twenty-First Century,* edited by William R. Farmer. Minneapolis, MN: Liturgical Press, 1998.

Niditch, Sharon. "Judges." In *The Oxford Bible Commentary*, edited by John Barton and John Muddiman. New York: Oxford University Press, 2001.

Olson, D. T. "Judges." In *The New Interpreter's Bible.* Vol. 1, edited by Walter Brueggemann, Walter C. Kaiser, Leander E. Keck, and Terence E. Fretheim. Nashville, TN: Abingdon Press, 1994.

Webb, B. G. "Judges." In *New Bible Commentary*, edited by G. J. Wenham, J. A. Motyer, D. A. Carson, and R. T. France. 21st century ed. Downer's Grove, IL: InterVarsity Press, 1994.

Works Utilized for Leviticus

Brown, Peter. *The Body and Society: Men, Women and Sexual Renunciation in Early Christianity.* New York: Columbia University Press, 1988.

Brueggemann, Walter. *Interpretation: Leviticus.* John Knox Press, 1982.

Cooper, Alan, and Susanne Scholz. "Leviticus." In *Global Bible Commentary*, edited by Daniel Patte. Nashville, TN: Abingdon Press, 2004.

Fox, Everett. *The Five Books of Moses: Genesis, Exodus, Leviticus, Numbers, Deuteronomy.* The Schocken Bible, vol. 1. New York: Schocken/Random House, 2000.

Gorman, F. H. “Leviticus.” In *The Harper Collins Bible Commentary*, edited by James L. Mays. New York: Harper San Francisco, 2000.

Grabbe, Lester L. “Levitucus.” In *The Oxford Bible Commentary*, edited by John Barton and John Muddiman. New York: Oxford University Press, 2001.

Hartley, John E. *Leviticus.* Vol. 4 of *Word Biblical Commentary.* Waco, TX: Word Books, 1992.

Haynes, Stephen R. *Noah's Curse: The Biblical Justification of American Slavery.* New York: Oxford University Press, 2002.

Houston, Walter J. “Leviticus.” In *Eerdmans Commentary on the Bible,* edited by James D. G. Dunn and John W. Rogerson. Grand Rapids, MI: William B. Eerdmans, 2003.

Kaiser, W. C. “Leviticus.” In *The New Interpreter's Bible.* Vol. 1, edited by Walter Brueggemann, Walter C. Kaiser, Leander E. Keck, and Terence E. Fretheim. Nashville, TN: Abingdon Press, 1994.

Levoratti, Armando J. “Leviticus.” In *The International Bible Commentary: A Catholic and Ecumenical Commentary for the Twenty-First Century,* edited by William R. Farmer. Minneapolis, MN: Liturgical Press, 1998.

Ringe, S. H., and C.A. Newsom. “Leviticus.” In *Women's Bible Commentary.* Louisville, KY: Westminister John Knox Press, 1988.

Pigott, Susan M. “Leviticus.” In *The IVP Women's Bible Commentary*, edited by Catherine Clark Kroeger and Mary J. Evans. Downer's Grove, IL: InterVasity Press, 2002

Watts, James W. “Leviticus.” *Mercer Commentary on the Bible*, edited by Watson E. Mills and Richard F. Wilson. Macon, GA: Mercer University Press, 1995.

Wegner, Judith Romney. “Leviticus.” In *Women's Bible Commentary*, edited by Carol A. Newson and Sharon H. Ringe. Louisville, KY: Westminster John Knox Press, 1998.

Wright, C. J. "Leviticus." In *New Bible Commentary*, edited by G. J. Wenham, J. A. Motyer, D. A. Carson, and R. T. France. 21st century ed. Downer's Grove, IL: InterVarsity Press, 1994.

Works Utilized for Romans

Achtemeier, Paul J. *Romans: Interpretation: A Bible Commentary for Teaching and Preaching*. Atlanta, GA: John Knox Press, 1985.

Bray, Gerald, ed. *Ancient Christian Commentary on Scripture, New Testament.* Vol. 6, *Romans*. Downer's Grove, IL: InterVarsity Press, 1998.

Byrne, Brendan. *Romans.* Vol. 6 of *Sacra Pagina*. Edited by Daniel J. Harrington. Minneapolis, MN: Liturgical Press, 1996.

Dunn, James D. G. *Romans 1–8.* Vol. 38 of *Word Biblical Commentary.* Waco, TX: Word Books, 1988.

Gaventa, Beverly Roberts. "Romans." In *Women's Bible Commentary*, edited by Carol A. Newson and Sharon H. Ringe. Louisville, KY: Westminster John Knox Press, 1998.

Hill, C. C. In *The Oxford Bible Commentary*, edited by John Barton and John Muddiman. New York: Oxford University Press, 2001.

Jewett, Robert. "Romans." In *The Cambridge Companion to St. Paul*, edited by James D. G. Dunn. Cambridge, England: Cambridge University Press, 2004.

———. *Romans: A Commentary*. Edited by Eldon Jay Epp. Minneapolis, MN: Fortress Press, 2007.

Meyer, P. W. In *The Harper Collins Bible Commentary*, edited by James L. Mays. New York: Harper San Francisco, 2000.

Schreiner, Thomas R. *Romans.* Baker Exegetical Commentary on the New Testament. Ada, MI: Baker Books, 1998.

Temple, Grey. "The Biblical Case in Favor of Gene Robinson's Election, Confirmation and Consecration." White paper given at Holy Innocents Church, Atlanta, GA, September 11, 2003.

Wright, D. F. "New Rhetoric." *Dictionary of Paul and His Letters*, edited by Gerald F. Hawthorne, Ralph P. Martin, and Daniel P. Reid. Downer's Grove, IL: InterVarsity Press, 1993.

Works Utilized for First Corinthians

Barclay, J. "First Corinthians." In *The Oxford Bible Commentary*, edited by John Barton and John Muddiman. New York: Oxford University Press, 2001.

Barton, Stephen C. "1 Corinthians." In *Eerdmans Commentary on the Bible,* edited by James D. G. Dunn, and John W. Rogerson. Grand Rapids, MI: William B. Eerdmans, 2003.

Bassler, Jouette M. "1 Corinthians." In *Women's Bible Commentary*, edited by Carol A. Newson and Sharon H. Ringe. Louisville, KY: Westminster John Knox Press, 1998.

Collins, R. F. *First Corinthians.* Vol. 7 of Sacra Pagina. Edited by Daniel J. Harrington. Minneapolis, MN: Liturgical Press, 1996.

Conzelmann, Hans. *First Corinthians: A Commentary on the First Epistle to the Corinthians*. Hermeneia: A Critical and Historical Commentary on the Bible. Edited by George W. MacRae. Philadelphia, PA: Fortress Press, 1975.

Fiorenza, E. S. "First Corinthians." In *The Harper Collins Bible Commentary*, edited by James L. Mays. New York: Harper San Francisco, 2000.

Hays, Richard B. *First Corinthians: Interpretation: A Bible Commentary for Teaching and Preaching*. Atlanta, GA: John Knox Press, 1997.

Lambrecht, Jan. "First Corinithians." In *The International Bible Commentary: A Catholic and Ecumenical Commentary for the Twenty-First Century,* edited by William R. Farmer. Minneapolis, MN: Liturgical Press, 1998.

Murphy-O'Connor, Jerome. "1 and 2 Corinthians." In *The Cambridge Companion to St. Paul*, edited by James D. G. Dunn. Cambridge, England: Cambridge University Press, 2004.

Sampley, J. Paul. "First Corinthians." In *The New Interpreter's Bible*. Vol. X. Nashville, TN: Abingdon Press, 2002.

Works Utilized for 1 Timothy

Bassler, J. M. "1 Corinthians." In *The Harper Collins Bible Commentary*, edited by James L. Mays. New York: Harper San Francisco, 2000.

Dewey, Joanna. "1 Timothy." In *Women's Bible Commentary*, edited by Carol A. Newson and Sharon H. Ringe. Louisville, KY: Westminster John Knox Press, 1998.

Dibelius, Martin, and Hans Conzelmann. *The Pastoral Epistles: A Commentary on the Pastoral Epistles*. Hermeneia: A Critical & Historical Commentary on the Bible. Edited by Helmut Koester. Philadelphia, PA: Fortress Press, 1972.

Drury, Claire. "The Pastoral Epistles." In *The Oxford Bible Commentary*, edited by John Barton and John Muddiman. New York: Oxford University Press, 2001.

Guthrie, D. "1 Timothy." In *New Bible Commentary*, edited by G. J. Wenham, J. A. Motyer, D. A. Carson, and R. T. France. 21st century ed. Downer's Grove, IL: InterVarsity Press, 1994.

Hultgren, Arland J. "The Pastoral Epistles." In *The Cambridge Companion to St. Paul*, edited by James D. G. Dunn. Cambridge, England: Cambridge University Press, 2004.

Mounce, William D. *Pastoral Epistles.* Vol. 46 of *Word Biblical Commentary*. Nashville, TN: Thomas Nelson, 2000.

Oden, Thomas C. *First and Second Timothy and Titus: Interpretation, A Bible Commentary for Teaching and Preaching*. Atlanta, GA: John Knox Press, 1989.

Perkins, Pheme. "The Pastoral Epistles: 1 and 2 Timothy and Titus." In *Eerdmans Commentary on the Bible,* edited by James D. G. Dunn, and John W. Rogerson. Grand Rapids, MI: William B. Eerdmans, 2003.

Schroeder, Hans-Harmut. "1 Timothy." In *The International Bible Commentary: A Catholic and Ecumenical Commentary for the Twenty-First Century,* edited by William R. Farmer. Minneapolis, MN: Liturgical Press, 1998.

Towner, Philip H. *The Letters of Timothy and Titus.* Grand Rapids, MI: William B. Eerdmans, 2006.